PRAISE FOR *VOICES OF GOVERNANCE*

"Karen Kane has made a significant contribution to the area of corporate governance communication with boards and CEOs. In *Voices of Governance: Why Oversight Is Important to All of Us*, she has brought to light the sensitive issues affecting leaders who sometimes find it difficult to believe something needs to be improved. She has discussed these ideas with balance and candor that encourages solutions and improved outcomes."—Fred G. Steingraber, Chairman and CEO Emeritus, AT Kearney.

"Karen Kane offers insight into what has been happening in the world of governance and what needs to be addressed. She gives voice to the many participants in this national dialogue."— Margaret "Peggy" Foran, Vice President, Chief Governance Officer, and Corporate Secretary of Prudential Financial, Inc.

"Boards are recognizing that they are no longer anonymous—they need to address shareholders by responding to their issues and concerns. Their reputations are at stake. In *Voices of Governance: Why Oversight Is Important to All of Us*, Karen Kane offers insight into how they can engage in a meaningful way with the owners of the company and improve governance in the process."—John LaSage, Burson-Marsteller.

"We continue to preach the gospel of "Tell your story" when it comes to compensation. *Voices of Governance* offers a number of examples where boards can improve their relationships with shareholders by improving their communication. Karen Kane provides valuable insight in helping boards to more effectively engage with shareholders."—Michael Melbinger, Partner, Winston & Strawn LLP, author of *Executive Compensation* and *Melbinger's Compensation Blog*.

"Karen Kane's *Voices of Governance* provides a valuable resource through her study of best governance practices in the area of board communication. As the governance landscape continues to rapidly evolve, it is particularly relevant for directors to read what thought leaders are saying on this topic." —Alice Peterson, Director, Williams Partners, Patina Solutions, and the Chicago Chapter of the National Association of Corporate Directors.

Voices of Governance:

Why Oversight Is Important to All of Us

By Karen Kane

KAREN KANE CONSULTING

ISBN: 1470193256
ISBN-13: 978-1470193256

TABLE OF CONTENTS

Board Dynamics

Leadership and CEO Succession

Shareholder Issues

Ethics and Compliance

Reputation

PROLOGUE—
WHERE ARE WE AND
HOW DID WE GET HERE?

Until the financial crisis of 2008, corporate governance was a topic for policy wonks, activists and corporate raiders who invoked the phrase to advance personal, business and sometimes selfish agendas. If Sarbanes-Oxley was the remedy for the WorldCom and Enron scandals, it was to bolster the board's responsibility for providing oversight as well as new rules to improve audit and accounting practices. Yet SOX didn't prevent the global meltdown of 2008 when iconic companies failed, and the government was forced to bail out GM and AIG and the banking industry at the cost of billions of taxpayer dollars. Corporate governance returned, not as a fresh idea but as the 2,331 page Dodd-Frank Wall Street Reform and Consumer Protection Act. In this installment, boards were the problem and shareholders had to be empowered to hold them accountable.

Today shareholders are part of the governance conversation. Shareholders have morphed into stakeholders and even into protesters as "the 99 percent" prove that companies operate in a public domain. How companies behave has become a matter of public interest according to law professor Hillary Sale. In the "publicness" of public companies, the failure of officers and directors to govern in a sufficiently public manner has resulted not only in scandals, but also "in more public scrutiny of their decisions, powers and duties," Sale says.

Central to the success of modern business practices and financial markets is the idea that corporate governance practices will define how an enterprise is directed and controlled, and make changes needed to ensure that the interests of shareholders are looked after in a responsible, professional, and transparent manner. At the center of the governance system are boards of directors, elected and charged with exercising prudent oversight on behalf of shareholders. Oversight of the enterprise is intended to instill confidence and serve as a check on management.

The financial crisis that emerged in 2008 cast doubt on the foundation of the prevailing governance system – its practices, policies, and core assumptions. Business leaders, shareholders, politicians and a wide array of technical experts grappled first with the crisis itself, and now with the myriad problems that the crisis has left in its wake.

There's no escaping the scope – and the urgency – of the issues. Calling the Western economic and financial system a "precious machine," Dominic Barton, Managing Partner of McKinsey & Co., nonetheless argues that the prevailing model of capitalist business faces the risk of survival unless business leaders modernize the system in a way that includes both popular and political support.

In spite of the scandals, corporate disasters and regulatory attempts that unfortunately failed to prevent the crisis, corporations remain the best organization for managing complex and global businesses. But they have to do better.

The global economic crisis demonstrated that the financial system is an essential part of any market economy, but it is based on a complex and fragile network of trust, administered by corporate boards, which are charged with exercising prudent oversight on behalf of shareholders.

"Sunlight is said to be the best of disinfectants," said Louis Brandeis almost a century ago and many elements of Dodd-Frank requiring transparency support the former Supreme Court judge's view. Shareholders hope that directors are acting in their interest, but transparency and effective communication provide the proof that they are.

In spite of the colossal governance failures, however, the loudest critics of corporate boards do not advocate their elimination. Rather, the American Federation of State, County and Municipal Employees, AFSCME , the Council of Institutional Investors, CII, California Public Employees Retirement System, CalPERS, California State Teachers Retirement System, CalSTRS, the Corporate Library, and others want boards to provide greater oversight by asserting their independence.

To the say-on-pay advocates, an advisory vote on compensation reinforces the accountability of boards to shareholders but does not usurp board power. In fact, except in rare activist cases, shareholders do not want to take on the work of the board. They just want the boards to do the job for which they have been hired. Absent the board, who would shareholders hold accountable if they were empowered to directly approve executive compensation? It is ultimately boards rather than shareholders that must approve executive compensation decisions that bear some relationship to longer-term business performance, are aligned with shareholder interests, and are fully transparent.

That continued faith in the basic design of our business and financial governance system illustrates why Western capitalism remains for many as Barton says, "a precious machine." But the scope of the problems laid bare since the crisis began in 2008 is wide, with the roots of some issues dating back 20 years or more. Directors relinquished governance authority gradually. Since the early 2000s, the center of gravity for corporate responsibility and board oversight quietly shifted from the CEO, to the board of directors, the shareholder activists, and now, increasingly to government. Ten years ago it was easy for boards to ignore shareholder concerns and petitions as aberrations. In reaction, shareholder activists agitated for greater regulations to enforce their rights, and in doing so, launched a worldwide movement that has resulted in a gradual power shift and a more shareholder-centric world.

The impetus for this power shift was born in the accounting and auditing scandals dating back to Enron and WorldCom in the late 90s, followed by a litany of other bad behavior such as insider trading, backdating options, and earnings restatements—all of which made boards appear to be complicit in management's sins. In the recent global economic crisis, the reputation of corporate boards hit an all-time low. Either directors lacked the competence to understand the risk posed by complex financial instruments or they simply failed to reign in the risks inherent in a system where asymmetric information from the chairman/CEO limits the board's oversight capacity. The fallout from governance incompetence had huge costs, devaluing the pension assets of 57 million Americans who invest in public companies. Suddenly, the public at large saw that it had a real stake in corporate governance.

Boardrooms have changed—poison pills have largely been eliminated along with staggered boards. Plurality voting has been replaced by majority voting. The ban on broker voting eliminates the silent pro-management voting block. The SEC's requirements for greater disclosure regarding the structure of the board and the competencies of its directors have brought greater transparency. While most companies sailed through their required advisory votes on say on pay last year, those that fail to makes revisions based on shareholder input may find the Institutional Shareholder Services (ISS) fanning the flames of shareholder activism this year.

At the same time, the wheels have been coming off company growth machines. When consistent, profitable growth falters, CEOs have a tendency to turn to layoffs to improve balance sheets. Others hoard cash, or propose divestures and mergers to distract from the lack of innovation and growth. Such developments reveal that boards may not have been paying enough attention to productivity, quality, growth and risk management—mechanisms by which companies renew their businesses, pursue sustainable growth and mitigate risk. Boards must retain some responsibility when CEO turnover is abrupt, creates a public spectacle and there is no internal candidate ready to take the helm because the board should be paying appropriate time and energy leadership development and succession planning.

Voices of Governance describes the breakdown of trust and the critical role that corporate governance plays in getting it back. In these pages, governance leaders talk about the steps they are taking, recognizing the concerns that shareholders have about crony capitalism and bankrupt practices. It begins with board leadership in reinvigorating the organization, the processes and the committee roles as well as the competencies of the board members. Smart boards see the need to transform themselves into strong, highly functioning work groups whose members trust and challenge one another. Directors also need to recognize the role shareholders play: they are the owners of the company and board-shareholder engagement is an important element in keeping them invested. Most importantly, boards need to demonstrate leadership in providing effective oversight in representing the interests of shareholders, and to hold management accountable.

Greater scrutiny and a wider cast of stakeholders have changed the role of the board forever. Directors are expected to bring their relevant business experience and judgment to help companies execute winning strategies. At the same time, directors put their reputations on the line. The best directors engage directly with leadership to challenge and improve management strategies to protect companies against threats of rapid decline and sudden demise. Strong directors can serve as player coaches, helping management to seize the opportunities that can elude management in the daily fray of running the business. The best boards turn governance into a competitive advantage.

Yet companies do not operate in a vacuum. Time Magazine's selection of the Protester as "Person of the Year" confirms a dramatic shift in the world order—power as we have known it will never be the same. The public has embraced its role in the global conversation. They will not be ignored. The repositioning will play out over time as the protesters demand change. Clearly, the genie is not going back into the bottle.

And what about the younger generation? What is their view of how the economy works? Do they see value in investing in companies directly or through 401 K programs? What accounts for a preponderance of younger people in the Occupy Wall Street movement? There is cause for alarm when 20 and 30-somethings tell the *International Herald Tribune* just this winter that the reason for their protest is that "We've given up on trying to use our votes. It just doesn't make sense." When such a large segment of the population loses faith in the underpinnings of capitalism and democracy, it endangers stability and global economic growth.

There are many voices in the wide-ranging conversation about what broke down in the governance system, what needs to be fixed in order to restore confidence – and how to fix it. *Voices of Governance* examines the issue of oversight as expressed by governance experts from 2009 to the present. In many individual interviews, as well as commentary on critical presentations and publications, *Voices of Governance* presents a unique and ultimately optimistic picture of where we are and where we are headed.

A LOOK BACK:
WHERE DID IT START TO GO WRONG?

DIRECTORS, YOUR IMAGE PROBLEM ISN'T GOING AWAY
FEBRUARY 4, 2010

The current issue of Newsweek features an interview with John Gillespie, one of the authors of *Money for Nothing: How the Failure of Corporate Boards Is Ruining American Business.* The title alone is fairly daunting for directors who have served and are serving on boards. Even if the public at large doesn't read the book, the broad reach of *Newsweek* will brand boards as "inept."

Charles Elson, the corporate governance expert at the University of Delaware, traces the origins of shareholder activism to the anger that stemmed from shareholders who felt they were being ignored.

The truth is that there are strong, energized boards and business leadership dedicated to delivering durable, long-term value through sustained economic performance, sound risk management and high integrity, and through meaningful consultation with shareholders. But the new book paints a dark picture because so little was known about corporate governance until the financial collapse.

Good directors should be concerned about "Money for Nothing." If they thought the legislative changes were merely grandstanding efforts by politicians, they were wrong. Actions by the SEC and Congress reflect the general concern that governance isn't being carried out effectively.

Good boards are stepping up to the new environment to demonstrate that they can make corporate governance more effective to serve the company, its shareholders and stakeholders. It will take reevaluation and rededication.

In this era of transparency, everyone will be watching. The public won't settle for less than effective oversight.

DIRECTORS FACE A CHANGED WORLD
AUGUST 11, 2010

As Ira Millstein told directors on a recent NACD/Weil webinar on the Dodd-Frank Act, they must align with the owners of the company, the shareholders. He advised directors "not to make believe" or "live in a dream world" because governance power has already shifted to shareholders and it's not going to be the way it was ever again.

The context for this change is the "new normal", a term coined by economists that characterizes an environment of high unemployment, slow growth, consumer distress, overly careful investors and long-term owners who will seek growth where they can find it. This is a challenging environment in which to serve as a director.

Millstein sees the changes wrought by the Dodd-Frank Act as tectonic, making Sarbanes-Oxley look like child's play.

But directors shouldn't wait until the final rules of the Act are written. Rather, they should engage with their shareholders now. He cited the fulsome letter that the Prudential board wrote in the proxy, introducing their thoughts on compensation. While Millstein believes directors should know what their shareholders think, he doesn't believe that they have to agree with them. "Explain why the board has a different view. That seems to me perfectly rational."

He noted that there was a huge amount to do in communication with shareholders, and boards should get ready to engage. Now.

DODD-FRANK REFLECTS 'NEW NORMAL'—
"BOARDS ARE THE PROBLEM"
JULY 31, 2010

"We're seeing a sea change in the environment of shareholder empowerment," said Holly Gregory, Weil Gotshal partner and governance expert. "The Dodd-Frank bill accelerates a fundamental change, a new normal in the balance of governance power." She went on to note that the eighth anniversary of Sarbanes Oxley, enacted during the aftermath of the WorldCom and Enron debacles, boards were seen as the solution to the failures in corporate accountability. "In sharp contrast the new legislation reflects the view that boards are the problem and shareholders must be empowered to hold boards accountable."

Gregory made these remarks on a National Association of Corporate Directors and Weil Gotshal webinar attended by hundreds of directors on Friday as boards try to better understand the requirements the new legislation, which President Barack Obama signed into law on July 21, 2010.

"I want to emphasize that the theme within the legislation is that boards are the problem," said Gregory.

Boards are well advised to recognize that the implementation of the legislation will fundamentally change their interactions with shareholders. For directors who have eschewed any contact with shareholders, they must engage with shareholders in meaningful ways to elicit their support. The sooner and more intelligently this dialogue begins the better for them.

CEOS WANT EFFECTIVE GOVERNANCE, TOO
FEBRUARY, 2010

Perhaps the most surprising element of John Gillespie and David Zweig's book, *Money for Nothing: How the Failure of Corporate Boards Is Ruining American Business and Costing Us Trillions*, is the jailhouse interview with Dennis Kozlowski, who considers himself a victim of the times and a weak board. The authors conclude that the Tyco board had faded into irrelevance compared to "the power, prestige, and satisfaction provided by the acquisitions" that Kozlowski engineered.

It's clear that strong, effective boards are in everyone's interest. Directors who offer a strategic sounding board for management, and who bring to bear their wisdom and experience as the company encounters challenges, are to be highly prized.

It will take more than just committed directors to improve corporate governance. CEOs, whether they hold the title of chairman or not, need to make the investments in effective boards. In addition to their personal commitment to make the relationship work, they need to provide the resources and support to help directors be effective.

THE PUBLIC HAS AN OPINION ABOUT DIRECTORS
JANUARY 15, 2010

As directors read the landmark survey of Main Street and C-Suite undertaken by Directorship magazine and Deloitte in conjunction with Korn Ferry International, they will see that the public's opinion of them and their performance is not high.

Directors need to know what people are thinking and saying and why. The results from the first survey create a baseline drawn from "Main Street" — journalists, policymakers, analysts, members of the C-Suite, including CEOs and directors and more importantly, teachers, laborers, policymakers, doctors, students and community leaders.

Let's begin with the credibility of board directors and CEOs. While less than half, 43 percent, said board and CEO credibility was poor, 39 percent said it was only adequate and only 17 percent said it was good. Only 1 percent said credibility of boards is outstanding today.

To the question of how boards performed their role of oversight during the economic crisis, a whopping 57 percent said poor, while another 29 percent called their performance adequate. A mere 1 percent gave boards an outstanding rating and 13 percent said it was good.

What can directors do about these low ratings? The Directorship article suggests that directors need to communicate. Directors should

16

be willing to engage in a role that helps shape public opinion, says Korn Ferry's Steve Mader.

HOW 'FIRST LADY OF CORPORATE GOVERNANCE' SEES DIRECTORS
NOVEMBER 22, 2009

Nell Minow, editor and co-founder of the Corporate Library and most recently the subject of a New Yorker magazine profile, took to the podium for the opening of the International Corporate Governance Mid-Year Conference in Washington, and in her inimitable style called them as she saw them.

"Wall Street executives are no different than the welfare queens—they're taking our money," opined Minow. "They are capitalists on the way up and socialists on the way down."

Clawbacks are meant to be punitive, she agrees: "It's not your money—you didn't earn it."

In her view, too big to fail means the company is a utility and those who manage utilities need to be paid accordingly. Her view is that "too big to fail is really too big to succeed."

"Remember when we gave Chrysler $1.8 billion? We thought that was a lot of money. And Lee Iacocca wouldn't take more than $1 in salary until Chrysler was outperforming the competition. Let's remember what we learned from that."

Minow believes that outsized pay packages are a risk indicator, especially in the way they describe their programs. "Companies tell us that they have established principles and accompanying metrics. We like it when we hear that there are nine principles for compensation. We hear a number and the word, metrics. But then the next sentence is that the company will pay out IF any ONE of those metrics are met." Clearly, this is not what she had in mind.

"Boards are really asked to be disagreeable," says Minow. "It's the duty of the board to imagine the worst and deal with it, like a mystery novel writer."

In her brief remarks, Minow showed that she cares passionately about these ideas. "It's up to us to fix corporate governance. It's not the government but the boards and the shareholders. It's our responsibility for capitalism to work."

ADVOCATES FOR THE PUBLIC
AS WELL AS CALIFORNIA TEACHERS
OCTOBER 25, 2009

When Anne Sheehan, Director of Corporate Governance for the California State Teachers Retirement System (CalSTRS) speaks, companies in which the nation's 2nd largest public pension fund invests listen.

"This is a new era," Sheehan told the audience at the National Association of Corporate Directors. "The financial crisis of the past year has resulted in the erosion of the trust of the American public in business. We represent our members and beneficiaries but we also believe we are a proxy for the American public who invest in public companies."

To restore trust, companies need to operate with transparency, acknowledge the role of the shareholders and demonstrate that management and directors are accountable.

"We may be seen as activist shareholders, but our interests are aligned," said Sheehan. "We want to see companies maximize their value. If you do well, we do well for our 833,000 public school educators and their families."

DIRECTORS, THIS IS YOUR DEFINING MOMENT
OCTOBER 19, 2009

In the opening address for a corporate governance conference for the National Association of Corporate Directors on Sunday, William George, the former Chairman and CEO of Medtronic and director of ExxonMobil and Goldman Sachs, urged his fellow directors to seize the moment and take the necessary steps to speak and act on behalf of good governance.

Adapting his remarks from his new book, *7 Lessons for Leading in a Crisis*, George told directors that boards are in crisis, having lost the trust of shareholders and the public. "It will take nothing less than board leadership to face the reality, work in concert with other board members, figure out the cause of the failures and become transparent in their actions, because boards are in the spotlight every day." The good news is that if boards take these steps they can help to return the focus to the long-term health of companies for the benefit of community and shareholders.

IN SILENCE DIRECTORS CEDE
AUTHORITY TO CRITICS
SEPTEMBER 1, 2009

Ralph Ward of Boardroom Insider, asked how boards should handle the ban on broker voting.

Naturally, boards will want to analyze the broker element of the proxy voting for their company. Yet any outreach to shareholders by the board should begin with a board-shareholder communication plan. Boards need a written communication policy, as prescribed by the National Association of Corporate Directors and suggested in their Blue Ribbon Commission on Board-Shareholder Communication. What are the goals of the board's communication? Will they take a minimalist approach because there have been few shareholder petitions? Has shareholder communication to the board increased in the past year? What are their vulnerabilities?

Writing a board communication policy causes the board to think through these issues, enabling them to anticipate and avoid crises while protecting the company's brand.

Boards face other changes on the horizon including the shareholders' bill of rights and proxy access. By working through these issues, boards begin to come to terms with the changed world in which they are operating. Smart board-shareholder communication is one way that boards can retain and regain control rather than cede their authority to critics through silence.

BOARDS HAVE A WINDOW OF OPPORTUNITY
AUGUST 26, 2009

SEC Chairman Mary Schapiro sees proxy access rules as the way to give shareholders a greater say on choosing directors and a credible path for ousting boards. Directors have reason to be concerned. It's clear that some form of proxy access will pass. However, this is not a time for directors to wait and see. Rather, this is a clarion call for boards to respond strategically rather than wait to comply.

Wednesday's *Wall Street Journal* describes the campaign by law firms, associations and companies to derail or weaken the current SEC proposal, which makes it easier for shareholders to nominate directors. "Fight Brews as Proxy-Access Nears" outlines the changes that proxy access, or Rule 14a-11, would allow stockholder groups, whether activist hedge funds or institutional investors, to place a candidate on a company's proxy materials at the company's expense. Furthermore, all of the candidates would be listed together, eliminating the current practice of voters checking one box to vote for management's slate of candidates.

Boards have a window of opportunity to use communication as a risk management tool. How much better for boards to frame the conversation about current governance practices rather than waiting to react and comply with the new rules? Boards have worked hard to assemble the right expertise on their boards, but few shareholders know how the amalgamation of talent serves to bring diverse views and business experience to their oversight role. Directors are listed in the proxy and appear on websites. However, the information does little to highlight their unique talents. Many directors are fearful that proxy access will weaken their boards just when strong boards are needed most. There are a number of simple steps boards can take to convey to all shareholders the expertise and dedication of the board. Boards that seize the moment with a customized board-shareholder communication program will be well positioned when the SEC finalizes the proxy access rules this fall.

LEARNING TO LISTEN—A KEY ELEMENT OF SHAREHOLDER ENGAGEMENT

REVIEWING THE ANNUAL MEETING
JUNE 29, 2009

Many boards heaved a collective sigh of relief after this year's annual shareholder meeting. Many, but not all. At the Citigroup annual meeting, directors fielded questions for six hours, allowing shareholders to express their frustration and pain over the devastating loss in shareholder value.

Meanwhile, in Charlotte at the Bank of America annual meeting, shareholders stripped Ken Lewis of his Chairman mantle. Given these circumstances, most directors in this season of shareholder meetings felt lucky to escape with a random interruption by a shareholder gadfly or an extended question that became a chance to pontificate during the Q&A period.

Directors should not expect board/shareholder relations to snap back to what they used to be. Shareholders are likely to exert more influence given their success, and aided by an activist SEC chairman Mary Shapiro, determined to expand shareholder access to the proxy before the 2010 proxy season.

This is a time for directors to think through their vulnerabilities to determine if the company is at risk in the current shareholder environment. What issues are simmering beneath the surface? Most directors know. If they don't, these traditionally quiet months are a great time to anticipate shareholder relations for the coming year.

ARE DIRECTORS READY TO MOVE FROM INFORMING TO PERSUADING?
JULY 29, 2009

Directors remain reluctant communicators. For years they have operated from behind the closed doors of the boardroom. Yet, the failure of some of the country's most iconic companies, as well as the devastating losses in stock portfolios, have made investors wary: what's going on in the boardroom?

In an effort to restore trust in the financial system, SEC Chairman Mary Schapiro wants to increase transparency and the quality of disclosure along with shareholder access to proxy voting.

Most boards are providing good governance. Longtime directors may be puzzled by the scrutiny and concern. "Directors need the tools of a politician," says Stephen Davis of the Yale Millstein Center and a longtime observer and participant in the corporate governance community. "They've been able to assume support at annual meetings. That's not the case anymore, not after the crisis. If boards handle it right, they can win the long-term loyalty of their investors. If they establish solid relationships with long-term owners—typically investors with longer time horizons—boards have more freedom to plan for the long-term."

By tools of the politician, Davis is talking about persuasion, not just informing but rather respecting shareholder issues and concerns and responding appropriately. Not necessarily by doing what they ask but by providing an explanation of why a decision was made. Davis advocates that directors re-link with the owners of the company, the shareholders, a move that has long-term value for everyone. Accountability improves performance. He feels the single biggest motive for all the reforms of the past 25 years has been "a sense of voicelessness and helplessness" felt by major institutional investors.

The sooner directors see the opportunity and begin to take measured steps in crafting communication policies that meet the needs of their particular companies, the more directors become a force for restoring trust.

DIRECTORS NEED TO STEP UP TO SHAREHOLDER COMMUNICATION
JULY 4, 2009

In his entreaty to his fellow senators to support his Shareholder Bill of Rights Act of 2009, Charles Schumer notes that "one of the central causes of the financial and economic crises...is the widespread failure of corporate governance." As he summarizes it, "too many corporate boards neglected their most fundamental responsibility—to prioritize the long-term health of their firms and their shareholders, and oversee management accordingly."

Unfortunately, Schumer's words are also directed to a public that has precious little understanding of what directors do. Accustomed to carrying out their duties behind closed doors, directors must recognize that they are no longer invisible. Investors, who now include taxpayers, are all too willing to accept the image that Sen. Schumer and the media have portrayed. Smart boards are not only adjusting their activities to bring greater focus to risk management and oversight in the current crisis, but are finding ways to better use their board time in dialogue and discussion to ensure long-term shareholder value. This is a time of credible actions and the communication that plainly describes the actions boards are taking.

TOWARD A DIALOGUE WITH SHAREHOLDERS
JULY 22, 2009

In principle, corporate directors have embraced greater transparency and communication with shareholders through various organizations including the Business Roundtable and the National Association of Corporate Directors. Yet individually, most directors are reluctant to interact with shareholders. Many invoke (while secretly expressing gratitude for) Regulation FD.

"Communicating is not in our DNA," one director confided.

At a minimum, boards need to develop their own communication policies to establish "Rules of the Road." That is, what should individual directors do when they are called at home by shareholders? Who represents the board to the media and under what circumstances? How does the board get important third party information without it becoming adversarial?

Given the shift from a director-centric to a shareholder-centric world, boards would be well advised to commence discussions about their approach to communication as they begin to craft policies. In the meantime, shareholder expectations are growing.

COMMUNICATION REDUCES RISK,
CAN EVEN SAVE SHARE PRICE
JUNE 3, 2011

AFLAC Chairman and CEO Daniel Amos has long endorsed transparency. AFLAC was one of the pioneers in offering a non-binding say-on-pay (SOP) vote voluntarily in the spring of 2008, prior to the financial crisis and Dodd-Frank.

In his recent comments at a financial industry conference in New York he conveyed what his company has learned in practice. "What did we do wrong?" was their initial reaction when AFLAC investors asked for the SOP prior to the new regulations. Directors and management "came to the shared belief that investors should have the right to know how the compensation packages at a company are calculated."

In his view, lack of transparency has an impact on stock price because it creates uncertainty for investors. Companies should view say-on-pay votes as part of an ongoing effort to be more transparent with investors. AFLAC's conclusion is that open communication with investors and analysts is better for long-term growth.

LEARNING FROM ACTIVIST SHAREHOLDERS
OCTOBER 21, 2009

While Bonnie Hill has distinguished herself in many ways as a board member, it was her willingness to meet with shareholders that made her a leader.

"I have never had a shareholder group ask something that was inappropriate," said Hill. "They are aware of Regulation FD. We may not always agree but I think it's very important to listen and sometimes agree to disagree. We have learned so much from talking to shareholders. It's made us better directors."

Her earliest meetings with shareholders came about because of shareholder issues or concerns. Now, the company talks with shareholders when they want input. For example, when the Home Depot board was working on director succession plans, they contacted long-term, large shareholders for candidates to consider.

"We found that amazingly helpful, said CalSTRS Anne Sheehan. "It demystifies the process, which enables us to better support the company's long-term objectives."

Such proactive work has accrued to the company's benefit. "When you are in reactive mode, it is so much more time consuming," said Hill. With a more open dialogue, Hill says the board has more time to spend on strategy and other key issues. And it has added to a positive reputation for the board and the company.

THE IMPORTANCE OF FINDING COMMON GROUND
SEPTEMBER 10, 2009

In the face of the changes that are coming to corporate governance, boards would be well advised to begin their examination of the input they receive from shareholders and stakeholders by looking for common ground.

A synonym for input is contribution. Imagine if boards saw the comments and suggestions that they receive from shareholders as the way that shareholders want to contribute to the improvement and long-term strength of the company.

Trust fosters trust. If boards want to engender more trust among shareholders, they can start by trusting that their shareholders sincerely care about the issues they raise and want what's best for the company and all shareholders.

Boards that start with finding common ground with shareholders can then build outward. Neither directors nor shareholders expect to be in complete agreement. But such an approach is respectful and has as its goal the shared long-term health of the enterprise.

GET STARTED ON A BOARD
COMMUNICATION POLICY
JUNE 25, 2009

Board-shareholder communications begin with the board, which oversees management communications to shareholders. The board can also communicate directly with shareholders when needed.

As a result of the events of the last 18 months, however, boards of directors are moving to develop more formal board communications policies and schedules.

What types of issues must be considered when developing such programs? We provide the following broad considerations based on our own experience managing the board-level communications and publications:

1. Make communication a board topic to discuss:
   o Create an inventory of current methods of communications—both formal and informal—between directors and shareholders.
   o What developments in the past 18 months have changed these methods? Were there contentious elements in the annual meeting? Document any other communication-related problems or risks evident over the last 18 months.
   o Which shareholder communications are the boards currently seeing?

- Is the full board seeing all communication from shareholders? Or, is the board seeing only what the Board Secretary deems the full board should see?
- In this new environment, what is the board's appetite for communication?
  - What processes will be put in place to govern communication?
  - Will the board name a primary contact for shareholders?

2. Assess current communication with shareholders
   o Assess issues of public and shareholder concern through correspondence and interviews.
   o How does the company's communication compare with a peer company's communication with its shareholders?

3. Identify opportunities for the board to anticipate and manage shareholder issues and concerns.
   o As directors identify investor concerns, they need to do the necessary research to understand motivation and intent. What are the investor's holdings? What is the investor's history and time horizon? What has the investor done in other companies?
   o What research has the investor assembled in making his/her proposal? What research has the company done?
   o What is the board's position based on the shareholder input, the management position and additional research?

4. Develop an action plan
   o Designate the chairman, lead director or committee chairs as spokesmen.
   o Arrange for communication training. Even if the designated directors are comfortable with the press, the world has changed and the media has expanded to include bloggers and even twitterers.
   o Develop message points, ensuring that the board is speaking with one voice and with appropriate consistency with the company.

5. Execute
    o   Maintain communication as an agenda item until the board has successfully executed one element of the communication policy—a directors web page, a shareholders' meeting, or another board-generated communication.
    o   Evaluate the success and comfort of the directors.
6. Monitor and follow-up
    o   Test the feedback. How are investors and shareholders responding? What adjustments need to be made?
    o   What improvements does the board want to see?

SAY ON PAY IS AN OPPORTUNITY FOR BOARDS TO ENGAGE SHAREHOLDERS
MARCH 6, 2010

Over 60 boards have proactively adopted say on pay in addition to those institutions that are required to offer shareholders an advisory vote on compensation by virtue of the TARP funds they received. Congress has advanced legislation to mandate such advisory votes at all public companies. Clearly, the tide is with granting shareholders the opportunity to express their opinion about the board's handling of executive compensation.

An investor network comprised of public pension funds, labor funds, asset managers, and representatives of public companies formed a working group and spent almost three years studying the ramifications of a say-on-pay vote. The companies on this working group, including Intel, Prudential Financial, and most recently Colgate, have enacted some form of say on pay.

"Our intention is to hold the board's feet to the fire, so that they are asking management questions on our behalf to protect our interests," said Anne Sheehan, Director of Corporate Governance of CalSTRS. "There is a shift in communication responsibility; board members should talk to shareholders."

She recognizes that such dialogue with shareholders could be time consuming. Certainly boards should have some kind of mechanism to talk to their ten largest shareholders, she said. But smaller shareholders should have some kind of unfiltered access to the board, through a website or other method.

To the many boards that have been reluctant to adopt an advisory vote, Timothy Smith, Senior Vice President of Walden Asset Management says that the advisory vote has become a more normalized response to the executive compensation issue and is not the fringe idea it was considered to be several years ago. "There's a strong business case to adopt say on pay," says Smith. "It's a good defensive strategy and removes the potential for a conflict with shareholders."

To the boards that counter that such a vote doesn't tell the board anything, Smith responds: "Yes, an advisory vote is a simple yes or no. But you should know where your shareholders stand on your compensation issues. You should never be caught not knowing what your shareholders think. You should know that before the vote."

Engaging with shareholders on key issues is what boards should be doing anyway.

HAS GOVERNANCE BEEN WRONGLY BLAMED FOR THE FINANCIAL CRISIS?
DECEMBER 21, 2009

TK Kerstetter's program, This Week in the Boardroom, took an interesting look back on the events of 2009 that will impact boards and directors in the years ahead. Both Kerstetter and his guest, Scott Cutler, noted that corporate governance has been politicized and wrongly blamed for the financial crisis, but both see an opportunity for directors to focus on effective corporate governance and the key role that directors play.

To Cutler's concern that "the strongest voices in corporate governance are not being heard," we offer the suggestion that directors could use their strong voices to communicate with greater clarity, rather than settling for languages that only satisfy lawyers.

Both Kerstetter and Cutler lauded SEC Chairman Mary Schapiro, who has moved quickly to bolster the SEC's regulatory and enforcement powers. At the same time, she strives to communicate intent in all the "why" of the SEC's action.

Take the recent press release about increased disclosure: The SEC announced new "rules to enhance the information provided to shareholders so they are better able to evaluate the leadership of public companies." The rules "will improve corporate disclosure regarding risk, compensation and corporate governance matters when voting decisions are made," said Schapiro.

It's true that shareholders are a diverse group and it is not the job of the board to satisfy everyone, but listening to varied points of view always improves decision making.

EVERYONE'S HOT BUTTON: EXECUTIVE COMPENSATION

GET READY FOR THE 2012 PROXY SEASON NOW
JUNE 19, 2011

Attorneys Mike Melbinger and Erik Lundgren of Winston & Strawn offered a recap of the 2011 proxy season in a webinar this week. Melbinger produces the most-read blog on compensation issues. While only 35 companies received failed say-on-pay (SOP) advisory votes to date, Melbinger insisted that this proxy season was no walk in the park. Not only do shareholders have heightened disclosure expectations, but seven more provisions of Dodd Frank will be in effect next year and he predicts that ISS and shareholder groups will be more dogged in their pursuits going forward. He also noted that companies made extra efforts to achieve positive votes in 2011—more companies provided executive summaries in the CD&A and linked pay for performance. Many emphasized "get out the shareholder vote" including shareholder and ISS outreach.

"Tell your story" was the theme of the action items that Melbinger suggested. "Silence is not golden. Unless you affirmatively, unequivocally adopt best practices, unambiguously disclose them and beat ISS over the head with them, you run the risk that ISS and others will assume that you do not follow that best practice."

Now is the time for boards to review what they learned from shareholders—whether at the annual meeting, through proxy voting or shareholder outreach. As for compensation, get rid of the problems and follow best practices now.

ANOTHER WARNING: PREPARE NOW
SEPTEMBER 14, 2011

Given the dramatic level of shareholder approval for most compensation programs during the 2011 proxy season, many directors may be inclined to view the historic Shareholder Say on Pay and frequency of say-on-pay votes as over and done. They would be mistaken.

In Winston & Strawn's excellent eLunch (webinar) program last week, "Preparing for the 2012 Proxy Season: Governance and Executive Compensation Strategies," Michael Melbinger, Christine Edwards, Oscar David, Erin Stone and Erik Lundgren reviewed the past season and advised that this is no time for complacency. Boards should be reviewing what they learned from their shareholders and preparing for the upcoming season, which will feature more Dodd-Frank requirements in the CD&A and other disclosures that link pay to performance. "Prepare early. Think about it now. Tell your story," Melbinger told the audience.

The SEC wanted say on pay to cause boards to interact with shareholders. That's what happened, particularly for companies with contentious issues. Those that prepared executive summaries used charts and plain English to explain their compensation plans, and even those who filed supplemental materials were largely successful.

The curtain has been lifted. Shareholders have greater expectations for communication with the board, more involvement in governance. Smart boards will anticipate shareholder issues and minimize contentious issues. Don't wait for the 2012 proxy season. Begin now.

DON'T BE A 'SITTING DUCK'—ADVICE ON AVOIDING ACTIVIST SHAREHOLDERS
SEPTEMBER 2, 2011

Poor financial returns, low stock price, a board that hasn't changed for over a decade—these are some of the board characteristics that attract activist investors. To make the case for board change, the activists will attempt to draw a correlation between poor financial and operating performance with poor oversight as a way to blame the board.

In a Blank Rome LLP webinar, partner Keith Gottfried warned participants not to be that board. Conduct your own evaluation of the board's vulnerabilities: Has the board failed to hold management accountable? Is the compensation excessive? Does the board lack sufficient industry experience? Has the board explained how each director is qualified? Is the board lacking in diversity? Is the board sufficiently independent? Is there a perception that the board is not "fully engaged"?

Paul Schulman of MacKenzie Partners and Chris Cernich of ISS also participated in the webinar.

Shareholders are now part of the governance dialogue. Not only must the board carry out its duty of care to represent all shareholders, but they must convey inboard structure and leadership as to how the board governs. The webinar together with the presentation is posted on the Blank Rome website.

COMP COMMITTEE CHAIRS: GET HELP
SEPTEMBER 29, 2010

Among the many requirements for Compensation Committees under Dodd-Frank is the heightened independence standard they must satisfy for any comp consultants. The Comp Committee has the authority to appoint, compensate and oversee compensation and other consultants. For most board members, "other consultants" or advisors would translate as "attorneys." Yet, what a chance for Comp Committees to get some real communication help.

If ever there was a time for compensation committees to clearly and credibly communicate, given the scrutiny they are under for creating and approving executive compensation, it would seem to be this proxy season. The first step in say on pay would be for the committee to clearly articulate their decisions in arriving at the executive compensation decisions. It gives them an important chance to "tell their story."

"Directors must ensure that the CD&A—which is the primary tool for shareholders to understand executive pay—is straightforward, complete and written in plain English," said Warren Batts, veteran CEO, chairman, director and NACD "Director of the Year" in a blog on executive compensation. "In addition, directors need to respond to shareholder questions and concerns as quickly as possible. I have stood up as chairman of the Compensation Committee more than once to explain what we were doing and why—and never had a negative comment afterwards."

Compensation Committees that take the time to carefully explain the philosophy and background of its decisions is a sign of respect for shareholders. Getting advice on how clearly you've accomplished that assignment could be the most cost-effective risk mitigation tool of the season.

DIRECTORS HAVE AN OPPORTUNITY
FEBRUARY 1, 2010

The Deloitte/Directorship survey demonstrated that opinions from both "Main Street" — journalists, policymakers, analysts and the "C-Suite" including CEOs and directors as well as teachers, laborers, policymakers, doctors, students and community leaders, have a relatively poor opinion about the effectiveness of the current corporate governance.

Smart CEOs and boards will see this as an important opportunity to use the current proxy season as a way to reach out to shareholders in a credible way—by drafting CD&As in plain English that are designed to explain the board's philosophy in devising pay programs that reward performance rather than failure.

InterimCEO is a worldwide network of interim, contract and project executives. Their website has posted my comments on board leadership on their home page. The InterimCEO network serves as a rich resource for executives and companies that are looking for assistance.

FEINBERG'S APPROACH OFFERS
CLUES TO DIRECTORS
JANUARY 5, 2010

How many professionals take on a highly visible thankless task for no pay not once but twice in the most challenging decade?

Kenneth Feinberg managed to create a program that persuaded 98 percent of the 3,000 victims' families of 9/11 to stay out of court and instead apply to his fund while dispensing the $7 billion that seemed to satisfy almost everyone. Then, last year, he took on the job of administering pay for the executives of the failed businesses bailed out by taxpayers. Not only did he create a credible template, he also injected common sense into the way executives are paid.

Directors could take a lesson.

Who but Warren Buffett could describe the current practice of a fictional greedy CEO engineering the approval of his rich pay package by engaging the compensation firm of "Ratchet, Ratchet and Bingo" to prove to the board that he is worth it? Buffett, the Chairman and CEO of Berkshire Hathaway, takes $100,000 in pay and says he would pay the company to do the job. "It's a great job!" However, while he's been running Berkshire Hathaway, the ratio of top pay to average pay at public companies has multiplied roughly 11 times, from 24:1 to 275:1.

As Steven Brill conveys in his excellent profile of Feinberg in the New York Times Magazine, Feinberg shows himself to be a straight shooter, independent and fair.

That's what most shareholders are asking directors to be—independent and fair.

BOARDS AND THE CULTURE OF THE COMPANY

MERGING AN AIRLINE, CREATING A CULTURE
OCTOBER 12, 2011

Chicago's newest hometown CEO, Jeff Smisek took to the stage at the Executive's Club of Chicago and offered some simple lessons for creating a new culture for the 86,000 employees of United, the largest airline in the world. Yes, he addressed the huge challenges facing the enterprise: taxes, regulation, and a capital-intensive and labor-intensive business. But, he noted, if you get the culture right, everyone is focused on doing the right thing and United-Continental will not just be the biggest airline but the best—the world's leading airline.

Smisek acknowledged that mergers are difficult enough for employees, but if you have the same terrible boss after the merger that you had before the merger, it's not going to help you make the airline better. The new United has a new culture based on dignity and respect. "It's simple. It's what your mommy told you: 'Treat people the way you want to be treated and never tell a lie.'"

That culture will encourage employees to use their best judgment in doing the right thing—the key to being a great company. And, he's made it the responsibility of the top 700 leaders in the company to help him root out the bad bosses by tying it to their compensation.

His remarks were brief, the answers to questions candid and forthright and the warm welcome conveyed to audiences support that he's the man to get the job done.

WHY TONE AT THE TOP MATTERS
SEPTEMBER 22, 2011

In the face of whistleblowers, tone at the top of the company has never been more important. So is the board's role in both overseeing and monitoring the culture of an organization.

In a webinar, sponsored by Jim Kristie of Directors & Boards magazine andthe law firm Morvillo Abramowitz, Barry A. Bohrer and Richard D. Weinbergdiscussed "Internal Investigations 2011: What Directors Need to Know."

In light of the new SEC rules that reward whistleblowers with rich bounties, the renowned attorneys stressed the need for strong compliance programs and a corporate culture that encourages employees to report problems early.

Weinberg suggested that boards consider "prepared preliminary action plans," which could include how the board would handle an internal investigation, vetting outside attorneys and forensic experts in advance, along with discussions about whether they would delegate oversight of the investigation to audit or a special committee.

How the board handles the investigation is critically important in terms of disciplinary action. Did the organization self-report? Did they handle the investigation expeditiously and credibly? Did they engage independent help in the form of advisors, attorneys and forensic specialists?

Shareholders, employees and the public are watching.

RUMSFELD'S NEWEST RULE: CONTINUE TO TRANSFORM

JUNE 9, 2011

Former Defense Secretary Donald Rumsfeld told a capacity hometown crowd at the Four Seasons that every organization needs to continue to transform. In his appearance for the Chicago Council of Global Affairs, Rumsfeld discussed the complex situation in Pakistan, his book "Known and Unknown" and the way a number of American and international institutions don't fit our current information age and need transformation.

Rumsfeld calculated that he has lived through a third of our nation's history. As both the youngest and oldest Secretary of Defense, a White House Chief of Staff, Representative to NATO and four-term congressman from Illinois, he has been an active participant in that history. He took four years to write the book and digitized a portion of his archive and made it available on his website in conjunction with the book's publication. Since launching in February, the site has received over 18 ½ million hits. Access to such a rich trove of information shows that "decisions are made with imperfect information." The bestseller has been called the first memoir of the information age.

Many U.S. and international institutions date back to the Truman years, an inflection point at the end of WWII and the beginning of the Cold War. NATO, the UN, DoD, CIA and so many other organizations date back to those days. "We've been changing and the world has been changing. And we need to be comfortable that the rest of the world is not like us."

Rumsfeld's message was that all organizations need to continue to transform. He's led by example, making handwritten and typewritten memos and papers from his long government service available for everyone to draw their own conclusions.

CIRCUMVENTING THE WHISTLEBLOWER INCENTIVE
MAY 10, 2011

At the National Association of Corporate Directors professional training in Houston this week, a group of seasoned directors were discussing the pending Security and Exchange Commission's rules for the whistleblower incentives that would circumvent the company's own internal reporting processes.

The discussion centered on the role of the board in encouraging employees to use the internal system to report any concerns.

"We do employee surveys at our company," said Roberta S. Brown, a director at several regulated energy companies. "The HR Committee asked to see all the written comments that accompanied the surveys," she said, as a way to better understand employee issues and concerns. "And we learned that employees were impressed to hear we read them."

The board's action sent a message to employees that their opinions were valued and concretely conveyed that the board was concerned about employee sentiment on all issues. In that way, the board encouraged the use of the internal mechanism to report concerns. It also conveyed the importance of "tone at the top" in terms of the board's commitment to hear the employees' perspective on issues.

OPPORTUNITY FOR THE HP BOARD
AUGUST 9, 2010

After ousting HP CEO Mark Hurd for his indiscretion with a marketing contractor, falsifying expenses to conceal his relationship, and thereby failing to live up to the HP code of conduct, the Hewlett Packard board has a chance to demonstrate to shareholders and the public that they intend to revive and enforce "tone at the top" of the storied Silicon Valley company.

Hurd and his predecessor, Carly Fiorina, who was also fired by the board, brought new meaning to the HP Way. Certainly, it was a different company than when brilliant engineers and founders William Hewlett and David Packard were at work in the company. Their instinctive style of "managing by walking around" would be almost impossible to replicate. Fiorina, ambitious and eager to make her mark aggressively drove the Compaq merger while a subplot revealed that the HP board had its own problems as chairwoman Patricia Dunn stepped down facing felony charges. After the scandal, Hurd's success was welcomed even if he took a cost-cutting and execution style approach to management.

With Hurd occupying both the Chairman and CEO role, Robert Ryan has served as lead director since 2008. But it has been Marc Andreessen handling the Hurd resignation. As the founder of another storied company, Andreessen has the gravitas to insist on a leader that not only performs well but behaves well.

Andreessen is given to greater transparency as well as sensitivity to culture and a larger group of stakeholders including investors, employees and the larger public given that he is an under-40, wildly successful entrepreneur now leading a company that provides a platform for social networking websites.

Andreessen is the spark that HP needs at this time, setting the tone and communicating what the board is doing on behalf of shareholders and stakeholders.

BUSINESS OF THE BOARD

MID-MARKET COMPANIES NEED
INDEPENDENT DIRECTORS
AUGUST 23, 2011

In their excellent paper posted on the Newport Board Group website, Gary Kunkle and Mark Rosenman discuss the need for independent directors at private, growth-oriented companies.

Entrepreneurs, they say, "need to look beyond day-to-day operational firefighting. They need the timeliest, savviest, most reliable counsel about markets, trends and companies." The authors provide a helpful guide to the natural stages of enlisting advisory help. Sure, the entrepreneur can go it alone, but he or she is likely to fall victim to "myopic decision making to which nearly all closely held companies are prone." A private company may seek independent board members when it needs liquidity, but the right independent advisors can bring so much more to emerging companies. Not only do independent directors help the entrepreneur to develop stronger, more professional management, but they often oversee the creation of financial and operational controls. The presence of talented businessmen and women serving as independent directors also sends a message to world that the CEO entrepreneur is confident enough to challenge his thinking in growing a stronger company.

MAKING THE MOST OF 24 HOURS
AUGUST 6, 2009

Directors unanimously agree that the pre-board package is bigger than ever before: There's more reading. The detail is denser. And, the issue of risk permeates every subject. Is it any wonder that both the length and number of board meetings has increased for many boards?

What were once all day meetings three or four times a year—or 24 hours—have now expanded. There are more in-person meetings, more telephonic meetings, and many more formerly unheard of one-on-one inter-meeting calls with individual directors.

Andrea Jung, the Chairman and CEO of Avon, is also a director at IBM and co-lead director at Apple. She credits her director work in helping her to be a better CEO. One informs the other as she can look at issues from both director and CEO vantage points. "The hours and effort spent in board work has increased more than tenfold," she said on a recent Agenda panel. "It's not a comparison to ten years ago but two years ago."

She calls the interaction with her board "constant" and "very critical."

With directors giving so much of their time, have the agenda and board books been revised appropriately? Is the pre-meeting information presented in a way that sets up the discussion for decision? Is the agenda managed so that directors do not feel they "run out of time" to discuss the really important issues.

IT'S NOT JUST SOCIAL MEDIA; BOARDS NEED STRATEGIC COMMUNICATION
MARCH 5, 2011

Concerned about social media, a few boards have actively sought new directors with a social media background to bring that capability into their boardroom. A staff member of the National Association of Corporate Directors mentioned that directors are having a hard time because the candidates are generally in their 30s and 40s and directors worry about upsetting the collegiality of the boardroom. That is, how would a 30 or 40-year-old fit with a group of mostly older directors? In fact, boards are getting older. The number of boards with elderly members is growing because many boards are raising the age limit for retirement to 80 and some eliminating forced retirement altogether according to Joann S. Lublin in The Wall Street Journal.

Social media may be a helpful competency but so much of what is embedded in the Dodd-Frank Act is a call for greater transparency, better communication between directors and the shareholders who elect them. Social media is communication, albeit faster and user-generated. Since the concept of communicating directly with shareholders is a new concept, boards need the assistance of high-level communication strategists—either as board members or consultants—to help boards craft their own communication policy and get them ready for the dialogue shareholders are demanding.

What directors are really worried about is hijacked media where a company's asset or campaign is taken hostage by those who oppose it. Managing social media is rooted in best communication practices, including crisis management.

BOARDS CAN ENCOURAGE GREATER INNOVATION
DECEMBER 21, 2010

Boards need to help their companies grow. As Fred Steingraber and I note in our article, *What Boards Need to Do to Remain Relevant,* directors need to re-examine and even revise board committees and committee work to bring the level of attention that is required to better understand the companies they serve. While oversight of executive compensation has caused the greatest shareholder concern followed by too little attention to talent and succession management, boards have not been paying enough attention to productivity, quality, growth and risk management—mechanisms by which companies renew their businesses, pursue sustainable growth and mitigate risk.

Directors, please turn to the New York Times magazine of December 16 and read about Jump, a hybrid strategy firm focused on growth. Either charter a new committee to review organic growth targets and trends or add that to another committee's responsibilities. Innovation is what will enhance a company's and yes, even the country's success. Directors who understand the broader developments in products and services, markets and channels, geography and relevant resource requirements can challenge and expand management's thinking. This committee should oversee the due diligence related to acquisitions as well as post-merger audits. They would also be responsible for understanding and overseeing the targeted and actual growth in revenues from new products in the last three to five years.

STRATEGIC IROS PLAY IT SMART
APRIL 9, 2010

The Investor Relations function is a critical management resource, representing the company to the Street and keeping management advised about the interests and perceptions of major shareholders and financial industry professionals.

Of course, there's much more to being the Investor Relations Officer than supporting the CFO or making presentations at major financial conferences or even the daily routine of interacting with analysts and shareholders. Many IROs provide analysis and information to management about who is buying and selling the company's stock. They may hire a surveillance firm to assist, but they are front-line analysts, interpreting aggregated information and making strategic recommendations.

Amid increased shareholder activism, as well as regulatory and congressional proposals, boards increasingly want access to this information as well. Such requests offer the IRO a unique opportunity to not just respond to the board but to help them take the next step in achieving greater effectiveness with shareholders.

In this new era of transparency and disclosure, boards need to understand the quality of shareholder interactions and ensure that the company provides transparent, effective shareholder communication across multiple audiences, including investors, brokers, owner research groups, employees, customers, and the community and public at large. As a member of management, the IRO can provide intelligence on stock and investment strategies to the board; however, the larger issues of governance communication best practices require the perspective of an outsider. To preserve its oversight function, boards need an independent communication advisor to help them think through their communication practices.

The board-shareholder communication discussion begins in executive session. How will the work of shareholder communication be handled? Will it be a subcommittee of an existing committee? Is it naturally the role for the lead director or independent chair? Has she or he had media training? Does the rest of the board know how to handle telephone calls and other information requests by referring the inquiry to the designated board member? What kind of standard does the board want to establish in communicating with shareholders?

An independent communications advisor with governance expertise can facilitate the board's work in this area, bringing a unique skill set as well as an outside perspective. The consultant's corporate experience recognizes management's communication resources and expertise, balancing message consistency with the board's responsibility for oversight.

How would the board handle a corporate governance challenge? Advance planning is the key to avoiding or minimizing negative impact. The board needs to preserve its independence by deciding how it will engage with shareholders and the public—constituencies that have, in some cases, lost faith in the board's ability to provide oversight. In other words, decisions about board-shareholder communication must emanate from the board.

The IROs who see that the tide has turned in favor of empowered shareholders—shareholders who want and expect unfettered access to the board they elect—will recognize the importance of communication expertise for the board. By anticipating and meeting the board's need for communication help amid cynicism and increased scrutiny, they engage a powerful ally in the company's reputation. As the board utilizes communication opportunities and begins to develop shareholder loyalty, the IRO helps to build a base of shareholders who embrace longer-term investing.

STRENGTH IN ECONOMIC RECOVERY SHOULD
PROMPT COMMUNICATION
MARCH 2, 2011

Calling it the Council's "rapid response programming", Michael Moskow opened the panel discussion, *Economic Recovery: Bullish or Bearish?*, featuring Mark Zandi, chief economist of Moody's Analytics, David Hale, a Chicago-based global economist, and Nial Booker, CEO of HSBC North America.

The Chicago Council of Global Affairs, co-partnering with the CFA Society of Chicago, convened the session to discuss the current state of the economy.

While acknowledging that there remain challenges to the economy, Zandi expressed optimism by noting the way American businesses have dramatically improved their operations since the financial crisis, cutting costs and increasing productivity. "U.S. companies are making money everywhere," he said. "They've got their cost structure down and improved their unit labor cost, which is rising in other countries." And, he added, companies are in a historically strong cash position, enhancing their global competitive strength.

What an optimal time for companies to get ahead of the Dodd-Frank Act requirements to more actively engage with shareholders by taking steps now to convey how boards are providing better oversight, more engagement in corporate strategy and greater respect for the shareholders.

FEWER AND SIMPLER WORDS, PLEASE
NOVEMBER 10, 2010

If Charles Peter McQuaid had his way, proxies would be shorter and easier to read, rather than the wordy, complicated documents that today are mostly written by lawyers. Proxies would describe how companies pay for superior performance. The Columbia Acorn fund votes against dozens of stock plans a year—those that reward sub par performance with high pay.

Columbia Acorn may be different because they do their own homework, reading the proxies for every stock they own. The fund has a lower turnover than most—20 percent. "Compare that with a hedge funds that is 11 seconds," said McQuaid, President and Chief Investment Officer of Columbia Wanger Asset Management at an NACD panel on performance metrics and compensation this week.

In addition, McQuaid would like it to be easier to find basic information in the proxy that the small and mid-cap investor cares about: How many options are outstanding? How many options were awarded? How many shares do directors own personally?

With a 26-year career in the investment business, McQuaid recognizes that companies are competing for talent and are not adverse to high pay for superior performance. "Good management can add value to a company and increase shareholder return."

IMPROVING CIVIC DISCOURSE
NOVEMBER 11, 2010

While the editors of the Columbia Journalism Review are addressing the press in helping to rebuild the American conversation, their advice has value for all of us.

"Ideas, particularly political ideas, are meant to be shared, to redefine themselves over the blue flame of discussion...increasingly Americans live in separate information silos. In uncertain times the tribes gather close. People don't talk to outsiders."

The editors urge the press to help "rebuild the forum that makes democracy work by being its best self" by taking steps to "Ignore the bias bullies", "Stand up for facts" and "Return to deep reporting backed by institutional processes", which means "lots of feedback from near and far, fact-checking, copy-checking and double-checking, all part of the practical effort to publish something that is as accurate as possible.

"A massive retreat into ideological niches is hardly restricted to cable TV, and it doesn't help the nation address its challenges."

Amen.

THERE'S A LOT BUSINESS LEADERS CAN DO
APRIL 10, 2011

Dominic Barton, McKinsey's managing director, argues that capitalism is endangered unless business leaders take steps now to "modernize" the system. This "precious machine" and "the best economic system" requires both popular and political support.

Barton spent 18 months talking to 400 business and government leaders around the world to develop his Harvard Business Review article, "Capitalism for the Long Term."

McKinsey has posted videos of Barton discussing his ideas, as well as articles to encourage others to engage in the discussion. "There's a lot of things that business leaders can fix," Barton says in one short video. "We don't need the government to tell us what to do, but we need to get out there and move on it."

Moving on it requires adjustments, shifting from a quarterly to a long-term focus, serving stakeholders while building value for shareholders, and strengthening governance.

Pointing to the increased complexity of business, Barton observes that the current governance model was developed for another time 30 years ago. The biggest shift is that directors need to spend more time on board work to understand the business well enough to provide strategic advice. He points out that boards of private equity firms spend about 74 days a year; corporate boards spend 15-20 days, too little to provide the strategic help that companies need in a competitive, global and 21st century environment.

LEADING BOARDS BECOME MORE
ENGAGED IN STRATEGY
FEBRUARY 23, 2010

One of the findings from KPMG's recent 28-city Audit Committee Roundtable Series is that leading boards are becoming more engaged in strategy as they pay greater attention to risk.

As boards take a hard look at their risk oversight process, they naturally turn to the risk element of the company's strategy. The SEC's proxy disclosure rules will require boards to take a good hard look at how they oversee risk. "If there isn't a clear framework in place, that's probably job number one" according to the roundtable report.

As boards engage in risk discussions, they are becoming more insistent that management provide alternatives and choices regarding the company's strategy, as opposed to the "review and concur" approach of the past. In this way, some boards are helping to develop and determine the company's risk appetite.

As one director said, "It takes time, effort and calories to do this right, but digging into the strategy is the only way to really understand what risks the company should or shouldn't be taking."

Smart CEOs look to the board in the strategy process.

ANOTHER WAY FOR CEOS TO COMMUNICATE
NOVEMBER 30, 2009

CEOs need to see themselves as their own media company. It's not just about being interviewed by *The Wall Street Journal* or *CNN*, but framing the discussion you want to have and reaching out to your clients and customers in your own voice.

Write a blog. It gives you a chance to connect to your audiences in a very authentic way. It's about having a dialogue rather than a press clip.

Do it now. The field is yours: not many CEOs are blogging.

Blog to establish leadership. Blog to get customer feedback.

Start the conversation.

FACING AN UNCERTAIN PROXY SEASON
DECEMBER 1, 2011

Patrick McGurn, Special Counsel of Institutional Shareholder Services, offered his insights into his firm's recently published governance policy for 2012 in a Winston & Strawn webinar. He urged companies to tell shareholders about their outreach efforts, what actions the company was taking as a result of last year's shareholder votes on say on pay and other issues and how the board would adjust disclosure as a result. Most importantly, he advocated a proactive approach, not waiting for the proxy, but making supplemental filings now that could be re-emphasized in the proxy.

He saw the coming proxy season more like 2009, the depth of the downturn and the "high-water mark" for activists rather than last year's relatively easy proxy season. He noted the backdrop of a presidential election and the anger that is being expressed in the Occupy Wall Street movement.

McGurn advocated more engagement and reaching out to the second tier of the shareholder base. He noted that opposition has come from these groups in the past.

The goal of such engagement is a dialogue. Since the say-on-pay votes are advisory, it's making shareholders part of the governance process.

LEARNING TO WORK WITH AND
AROUND RISKMETRICS
NOVEMBER 4, 2009

Five years ago, Risk Metrics Group, now Institutional Shareholder Services, the provider of proxy advisory services, seldom heard from the directors of the boards whose governance they evaluated.

"These days, it's not unusual for a board member—typically the lead director or a key committee chair—to initiate the contact with RiskMetric's research team. It's common for a director to lead the discussion," said Patrick McGurn, Special Counsel, ISS.

These discussions typically focus on an issue upon which ISS will make a vote recommendation rather than a rating. "We've been encouraged by the broader response to the concerns we raise about governance," McGurn said.

Many directors were hoping that concerns over executive compensation would melt away as the stock market improved, but the populist outrage over executive pay has only increased, which is reflected in the government's growing intervention in the boardroom.

"Today, the government has its torso in the door, not just its foot," observed McGurn. If boards aren't responsive to shareholder concerns, they place the company's reputation, as well as their own reputations, at risk. "Investors expect boards to be more accountable because they see the directors as their elected representatives."

With say on pay and proxy access all but deferred for the 2010 proxy season, shareholder petitions and vote-no campaigns will be the focus. "Every director looks at the results of the vote-no campaigns," said McGurn. "The directors who have worked hard and anticipated the issues will have an easier time.

"As Warren Buffet said, 'When the tide rolls out, it's clear who's wearing a bathing suit.' And the tide has rolled out."

Said McGurn: "Smart boards that take control to improve shareholder engagement will be better positioned in this new environment."

BOARDS SHOULD SPEAK FOR THEMSELVES
SEPTEMBER 30, 2009

In light of the SEC's ban on broker voting, there is considerable concern about the conflicted business model of proxy advisory firms such as Institutional Shareholder Services, which provides proxy voting recommendations to institutional investors along with a proprietary governance rating, while an arm of ISS sells advice on how companies can improve governance scores.

Directors shouldn't spend too much time railing against these firms. Rather, it's time for boards of directors to bypass these groups and review their own governance policies (including charters, bylaws and compensation rules) so that they are well versed on the company's corporate governance policies. At the same time, boards should develop an understanding of their shareholders and their concerns.

With this knowledge, boards will lower their resistance to speaking out about the role they play in providing oversight. They will become "communication ready," willing to craft their own communication policy, a "rules of the road" so to speak that supports a customized and effective shareholder engagement program.

In the old world where directors were assured easy election, criticizing proxy advisory companies was easy sport. Today, boards need to speak for themselves; they must communicate their competencies and the attention they dedicate to the important work of representing shareholders and providing oversight.

BOARD MEMBERS CAN HELP
WITH STAKEHOLDER RELATIONS
DECEMBER 7, 2011

Maryann Waryjas of Katten Muchin and Gail Meneley of Shields Meneley Partners convened a group of non-profit board members and supporters to a breakfast panel discussion, "Stepping Up to Leadership: What Nonprofits Need from Board Members" featuring Francesca Edwardson, CEO of the American Red Cross of Greater Chicago, Ricardo Estrada, CEO of Metropolitan Family Services, and Richard Malone, CEO of YMCA of Chicago. David Coolidge, vice-chairman of William Blair and a veteran director of 28 non-profit and public company boards, served as moderator.

Malone spoke of the importance of board members helping with external stakeholder relations, especially in the way the organization should be perceived by the community, bringing important information back to leadership. Edwardson spoke of her pride in being a servant to the Red Cross and how important it was for directors to bring their passion to a non-profit board. Estrada spoke of the value of director expertise to fill in gaps of knowledge and expanding the network of the non-profit.

Since fundraising is an important element of non-profit board duties, all three leaders spoke about their concern of losing a strong board member, either through term limits or retirement. Yet these leaders said they've learned to have faith in their board's nomination and governance committees or leading directors. Their thoughtful and proactive efforts identify new talent to renew the board with new skills that help contribute to the longevity of the organization.

BOARD DYNAMICS

HOW CEOS AND BOARDS CAN ENSURE CONSTRUCTIVE TENSION
JUNE 1, 2011

In a National Association Corporate Directors webinar, Ken Daly, president of NACD, Kenneth Duberstein, lead director of the Boeing Company, director of Conoco-Phillips and The Travelers Companies, and Stuart R. Levine, director of Broadridge Financial Solutions and lead director of J. D'Addario & Company addressed the thorny issue of trust between the CEO and the board.

Using the example of his work as CEO of NACD, Daly demonstrated how important it is for CEOs to invite candid dialogue from the board. "Trust is built over time and developed through actions, not words. The way to develop trust is for the board and management to recognize that they are on the same team, that communication is straight-forward, two-way and straight from the horse's mouth." It's also important to telegraph emerging issues. Duberstein noted that management and boards are on the same team but have different roles—management is charged with execution and the board needs to actively participate in strategy decisions and provide oversight for all shareholders by monitoring performance and asking the right questions.

Properly managing executive sessions and giving good feedback to the CEO was discussed. Levine, a best-selling business author, noted that the CEO of Broadridge has a practice of calling each board member prior to the meeting to get a sense of the board's issues and concerns. "That way, we're already engaged before the meeting."

What the discussion among these leaders with broad experience emphasized was how important it is for both boards and CEOs to "get it right." The webinar provided valuable insight.

CRITICAL DIALOGUE BETWEEN
AUDIT COMMITTEES AND CFO
JUNE 24, 2011

In a webinar that provided significant information about the increasing responsibilities for audit committee members, KPMG's Audit Committee Institute and the National Association of Corporate Directors featured Carol B. Tomé in a webinar on June 23. Not only is Tomé Home Depot's chief financial officer (CFO), she also serves as chairman of the audit committee in her board role at UPS. James P. Liddy, Vice Chair of Audit, KPMG, moderated the webcast, which provided updates on key financial reporting/accounting developments, including FASB projects and "hot button" issues. Asked what advice Tomé would give to CFOs she said,

"Remember, it's not a parade ground presentation—don't spend excessive time on your slides." It's the engaged dialogue between the CFO and the audit committee that will really pay dividends. "Begin by thinking of the outcome you want and measure yourself against it." As for what audit committee members need to do to make the most of their interaction with the CFO, Tomé emphasized the need for interaction prior to the meeting. Having a relationship with the CFO beyond just the board and audit committee meeting is critical. "It's important to have that up front communication prior to the meeting," she said. Such conversations enable the CFO and audit committee to know what the issues are and where you should spend your time together. "Yes we have different roles but we're all working for the shareholders."

BOARD OVERSIGHT OF RISK REQUIRES CANDOR
MAY 15, 2011

"Collegiality can be the enemy of good board governance," said Christine A. Poon during a National Association of Corporate Directors Chicago Chapter seminar on Global Boards and International Risk Management. She is Dean (and John W. Berry Chair) in the Max M. Fisher College of Business at Ohio State University and board member of Prudential Financial and Philips Electronics in the Netherlands. She was formerly Vice Chairman of Johnson & Johnson.

Boards must get the information they need and engage in rigorous discussion when it comes to oversight of a company's risk management and growth. "There's no need to be disrespectful, but it is critical that directors get the answers they need to understand the issues."

Fellow panelist Lisa A. Payne concurred. "You have to train management to eliminate the mind-numbing presentations that go out in the board books and tell them that management should come to the board with a handful of overheads so that we can use our time together to get to the heart of the matter." She is Vice Chairman and Chief Financial Officer of Taubman Centers, Inc., a director of Masco Corporation and Taubman and a trustee of the Munder Funds.

Executive session is a key tool for the board. "We often begin with an executive session," said Payne. "It enables us to focus on the key issues through the duration of the meeting. We often meet again in executive session after the formal meeting."

CEOS, HELP YOUR BOARD PREPARE
FOR PROXY SEASON
SEPTEMBER 17, 2010

Dear CEO,

Have you given your board the tools it needs to navigate the coming proxy season? It's up to you to see that your board is prepared.

The Dodd-Frank Act creates new requirements for board disclosure and greater transparency. Governance power has shifted to shareholders, who are now empowered to hold boards and management accountable. How your board moves forward in this new environment is critical.

CEOs need to see their boards as helping them to restore confidence in the system. If you wear the mantle of both CEO and chairman, it's even more critical that you set the tone for clear disclosure and genuine engagement with shareholders. This sends a signal that you respect their importance in the long-term health of the organization.

The new disclosure rules encourage boards to build trust with shareholders through the application of sound principles, transparent communications and actively engaging with them to secure a favorable vote. Board members will need to become better communicators. But they need guidance in demonstrating independence and credible oversight. Some basic communication planning should begin now.

What may prove to be a best-in-class approach is for the board to articulate its principles, its own "Articles of Governance", to serve as the source for board communication and shareholder engagement. By reviewing its current identity, which resides in governance and legal documents, the board can craft a comprehensive board governance doctrine that prepares the board for the upcoming proxy season and beyond.

This proactive approach enables the board to discuss and decide in advance how it will handle critical issues. By working through issues in an atmosphere of calm, the board is better prepared to face a crisis and even avoid or mitigate one.

Disclosure in governance is an area we understand well and we would be happy to assist you.

DOES "CORPORATE DEMOCRACY" MEAN DYSFUNCTION?

JULY 29, 2010

With the passage of the Dodd-Frank Wall Street Reform and Consumer Protection Act, board service organizations are conducting webinars to help directors understand the changes. The director moderating a recent session seemed particularly out of touch as noted that it was difficult for shareholders to nominate their own directors, but said it was unclear to him why it was a problem and why Congress had done anything to authorize the SEC to change the rules.

"I'd hate to think that the U.S. corporate world will become as dysfunctional as the U.S. Senate," he said, referring to "this monstrosity" of legislation. His questions to his fellow panel members reflected his belief that new regulations were going to stifle performance. "This is meant to encourage dialogue with shareholders, which is an important principle of the legislation," the panelist replied.

It turns out the moderating director has the educational and legal experience that boards seek. But he's 70 years old. He has served on his current board since 1977. The other director who joined the board with him is 86 and a third director, who is 83, joined the board in 1959. There are younger board members—74, 62, 52 and 46. But clearly, this is a board that needs to renew itself.

The world has changed. Board work has changed. It requires recognition of the important role that shareholders play in governance. The director may be an esteemed professional, but he has missed the last ten years of shareholder activism, brought about because boards turned a deaf ear to shareholders.

CEOS, DIRECTORS AND LAKE WOBEGON
MAY 11, 2010

While the news is full of reports about shareholder concerns over the quality of corporate boards, it turns out that CEOs have questions, too.

It's the Lake Wobegon syndrome where 95 percent of directors think they're doing a good job. CEOs see it differently. According to work by Heidrick & Struggles, CEOs "almost universally confide" that they have one or two directors who provide wide counsel, offer advice on key issues and contribute both formally and informally to the enterprise. That means that 80 percent of the directors are seen as not being very effective by the CEO.

The fictional town of Lake Wobegon, where "all the women are strong, all the men are good looking, and all the children are above average," has been used to describe a real and pervasive human tendency to overestimate one's achievements and capabilities.

CEOs need to see their boards as providing a competitive advantage to them and their enterprise. If board members are less effective, the board needs to replace them. Without outside help, CEOs and other directors find it hard to ask less effective directors to leave.

CEOs need to ask, are they giving their boards the right tools to be effective? Is management teeing up information for decision, providing the context and the why for the company considering it? Or, do boards get a fire hose of information or worse yet, only the information that management wants them to see? Are boards spending their time on the right issues? Do boards have access to tools and advisors to make them more effective?

Boards are working harder than ever. CEOs need to see to it that the board has the resources it needs to create strong work groups.

While the news is full of reports about shareholder concerns over the value their elected representatives, the board of directors, bring to the enterprise, it turns out that CEOs have questions, too.

LEADERSHIP AND CEO SUCCESSION

VALUES AND BEST PRACTICES IN CEO SUCCESSION MANAGEMENT
AUGUST 17, 2011

In its webinar on *CEO Succession and Compensation* co-sponsored by NACD, Pearl Meyer & Partners Yvonne Chen and Matt Turner discussed the growing visibility and importance of the CEO succession process and effective compensation practices. The issues abound, whether it's the board's oversight role in developing strong internal candidates for the job, having an immediate successor in place in case of an emergency, or keeping those "runner ups" engaged in the company even if they are not selected for the post. High-profile CEO succession failures have a demonstrated negative impact on the company's stock and create a host of challenges related to employees and public relations. Moreover, it is clear that when a company goes "outside" to find a new CEO, it's more costly—79 percent of those CEOs who are paid more at target than the prior CEO are external hires.

One of the questions posed during the webinar was about the performance of internally developed CEOs versus externally recruited CEOs. A recent study by the Kelley School of Business of Indiana University, led by Fred Steingraber, directly addresses this question. An article outlining the study's findings (co-authored by me) appeared in a recent issue of Corporate Board Magazine. The study, which details the superior performance of internally developed CEOs, examined the leadership of the most successful non-financial

S&P 500 companies from 1988 through 2007. The 20-year duration was critical to the study because it minimized distortions of performance that could have occurred over shorter time spans of three, five or even 10 years. In addition, this two-decade period was characterized by different economic cycles, globalization, dramatic technology advances, shifting consumer preferences and changes in leaders competing under a wide variety of conditions.

In our article, we summarized how this group of 36 S&P 500 non-financial companies was distinguished by consistent, superior leaders over the 20-year span, outperforming the remaining S&P 500 firms in seven measurable metrics: return on assets, equity and investment, revenue and earnings growth, earnings per share (EPS) growth and stock price appreciation.

We believe this study demonstrates the ability of "home-grown leadership" to consistently generate superior results and the importance of the board's focus on effective CEO succession.

HOW DIRECTORS CAN ASSESS RISK (AND LEARN MORE ABOUT THE COMPANY'S TALENT)
OCTOBER 18, 2010

Ed Breen became the Chairman and CEO of Tyco after the disastrous leadership of Dennis Kozlowski, who said from prison that his board "didn't get in his way." After convincing Kozlowski's board not to stand for re-election, Jack Krol, the former CEO of DuPont, became lead director of Tyco and worked with Breen to recruit a new board that could work effectively as a team and serve as a competitive advantage to the company.

In the tumult of change, Krol was concerned about the company's risk and proposed that he and members of the board visit every division of Tyco, talk to the leadership and build a risk profile of the company, an enterprise-wide assessment. Not only were the board members able to develop an assessment of the company's risk, but in the process, board members got to know the next level of leadership in the company. Tyco divisional management liked the unfettered access to the board. Of course the company had its own risk assessment process and they are currently combining the two.

It's not easy to take on such a task. But after developing a process and executing on it, the board came to a deeper understanding of the company. Directors like Jack Krol, willing to spend the time and energy to help a company recover and become better, bring real value to shareholders.

DIRECTORS NEED TO APPLY "BUSINESSLIKE" VIEW
DECEMBER 27, 2009

The two studies cited in The Wall Street Journal remind directors that they should be both independent and "businesslike" when it comes to evaluating management. Two new studies challenge the notion that companies that pay top price get top talent. Lucian Bebchuck's Harvard study pointed out that the bigger the "CEO pay slice," the lower the company's future profitability and market valuation. Adding fuel to the fire is the study by finance professor Raghavendra Rau of Purdue, who looked at CEO pay and stock returns for roughly 1,500 companies. The conclusion of his study: 10 percent of firms with the highest-paid CEOs produce stock returns that trail their industry peers by more 12 percentage points, cumulatively, over the next five years.

Clearly, one issue for shareholders during the 2010 proxy season is how the board provided oversight for CEO compensation. In 1951, legendary investor Benjamin Graham suggested that directors submit to an interrogation in order to justify "the generous treatment" they are asking shareholders to approve. "The stockholders are entitled to be told...just what are the excellent results for which these arrangements constitute a reward, and by what analogies or other reasoning [has] the board determined the amounts accorded are appropriate?"

Surely such questions are valid 59 years later.

SHAREHOLDER ISSUES

DIVERSITY—ACKERMANN'S COMMENTS COULD PROMPT QUOTAS

FEBRUARY 9, 2011

When Deutsche Bank Chief Executive Josef Ackermann said he hoped "someday" his board would be "more colorful and prettier, too," it sparked new discussion about new regulations and even quotas. Angela Merkel opposes quotas for the number of women on boards, even though Germany has the poorest track record in Europe for female representation. France passed a law this year requiring companies with more than 500 employees and more than $68 million in sales to have women in 40 percent of the supervisory board positions within six years. Spain has the same requirement. Women remain a minority in the boardroom in the U.S. (15 percent) and the UK, where it has stagnated at 12.5 percent for the third year running.

It might be well for U.S. directors to consider that governance concepts that originate outside of the U.S. have a history of moving into the American mainstream rather quickly. Consider "Shareholder Say on Pay," which began when U.K. cabinet minister Stephen Byers' 1999 white paper suggesting that shareholders have a more active role in overseeing companies by requiring a "non-binding shareholder advisory vote on remuneration." In 2002, the U.K. government adopted the Directors' Remuneration Report Regulations, which made annual pay votes mandatory. By 2004, say on pay spread to continental Europe as the Netherlands made it a requirement; it moved to Norway, Sweden, Spain, Portugal, Denmark, France, Germany and Australia before institutional investors in the U.S. filed shareholder proposals at 44 companies by 2007. Just last week, the SEC finalized the rules on say-on-pay and say-on-golden parachute rules.

Diversity is on the minds of American directors, according to the recent PwC's Annual Corporate Directors Survey with 45 percent of them citing the difficulty in finding qualified candidates of diverse gender, race and with expertise in technology. A whopping 86 percent of directors say they use their own network of contacts to recruit new board members. Given the possibility of quotas for women on U.S. company boards and the new rules for greater transparency in describing the competencies of every board member, directors are well advised to look more broadly for board candidates, or shareholders may propose their own candidates in proxy access.

COURT STALLS IMPLEMENTATION
OF PROXY ACCESS
JULY 25, 2011

The US Chamber and others cheered the decision of the US Court of Appeals in overturning "proxy access," which would have given large shareholders the right to nominate their own slate of directors. However, it would be wise for sitting directors to think beyond the safety of their own board terms.

In rushing to get the rule in place, the SEC failed to "determine the likely economic consequences" of the rule and its effect on "efficiency, competition and capital formation"— all of which it must do by law.

But directors should consider the level of shareholder concern about their governance record and not just the unions that are seeking increased benefits. Creeping federal regulation is the result of "corporate officers and directors not doing their jobs," according to Hillary Sale in her paper, "The New 'Public' Corporation." "They have failed to understand the force of public scrutiny and have, thereby, failed their corporations. They are not good public company stewards."

The message to companies about the past ten years of increasing shareholder power is that shareholders are part of the governance conversation. Whether the SEC redoes its analysis and reissues its rule, corporate directors would do well to consider the level of shareholder disappointment that helped create Dodd-Frank and develop more effective board-shareholder engagement to satisfy and encourage long-term investment and participation.

UNIONS AND THE NEED TO COMMUNICATE
THE BENEFITS OF FREE TRADE
DECEMBER 10, 2010

Major unions were quick to criticize the proposed U.S.-South Korea free-trade deal, complaining that the deal will drain manufacturing jobs and insisting that Congress nix the deal because it does not include worker protections.

What a shame!

Just a few weeks ago, a number of CEOs gathered to discuss their agenda for dealing with the sluggish economy and other key challenges in a Wall Street Journal CEO Council. Their view was the need for "jobs, jobs, jobs" to get the economy moving. Doesn't that sound like business and unions are on the same page?

"If the U.S. wants sustainable job growth, it must strongly embrace global trade," the CEOs concluded.

In the meantime, "free trade" has become a toxic term. Like it or not, the U.S. competes in a global marketplace. Business and government need to join forces to foster broader understanding that there are benefits for the U.S. to engage globally. At the same time, business needs to do a better job explaining what they are doing well in the international market and how it benefits consumers.

The truth is that there is no turning back to isolation and protectionism. "Rebuild the consensus around free trade by emphasizing the benefits to the developed world. Encourage the flow of intellectual capital through immigration and across borders.

Business should talk more about the jobs created from trade and the benefits to consumers."

Communication can help to open minds to the benefits and opportunities of a global environment

HOW WILL DIRECTORS RESPOND
TO SEC'S BROKER-VOTE RULE?
JULY 13, 2009

The SEC's July 1 decision to eliminate broker discretionary voting in directors' elections could have significant consequences when it takes effect in the 2010 proxy season. In a press release last week, the Conference Board suggested that board members analyze the company's current vulnerabilities with regard to activist investors and to **"regularly communicate** in compliance with Regulation FD and insider trading rules with the 10 largest institutional shareholders to inform them of the business strategy, including new efforts for improving shareholder value."

It's not just the company's top ten shareholders who are watching. In the face of the economic crisis and the ongoing volatility of the financial markets, doesn't it make sense for the board to communicate what they do to provide oversight, represent all shareholders and add value? After all, it's the individual board members who will face "no" votes and risk failing to be elected.

The world has changed. Directors can no longer operate from behind the curtain and expect that shareholders will understand that they are doing their jobs. Directors have an opportunity to educate the less sophisticated investor and reassure the public at large that they take their responsibility seriously. By communicating appropriately, directors show respect for shareholders and keep them invested in the company.

INVESTOR GROUPS SEE ANNUAL MEETINGS AS FORUMS FOR DIRECTOR ACCOUNTABILITY
MARCH 22, 2010

According to the Washington Post, investor groups are staging a two-pronged attack against lax corporate governance: they are pushing for legislation that gives shareholders more power, and they will use shareholder meetings as a forum for holding directors accountable for oversight.

Proposals being submitted for inclusion in upcoming company proxies include the following:

- The right to call a special meeting
- Independent board chairman
- The end of the supermajority vote requirement
- Say on pay
- Review/report on political spending

Over 60 boards have proactively adopted say on pay in addition to those institutions that are required to offer shareholders an advisory vote on compensation by virtue of the TARP funds they received. How involved is the board in writing and reviewing the proxies? What do they know about the sentiment of their shareholders on these issues?

In the current environment, boards should be actively engaging with shareholders.

AFTER 452, IT'S TIME FOR CREATIVE OUTREACH TO SHAREHOLDERS
MARCH 1, 2010

With the election of board directors too important to be considered routine, NYSE Rule 452 was amended to eliminate broker voting, thereby removing typically management-friendly broker votes from director elections this year.

But if shareholder voting on the election of directors is viewed as a critical component of good governance, how do you get registered shareholders to vote?

The Securities and Exchange Commission has launched an investor-focused website to help consumers invest wisely and avoid fraud. The site, www.Investor.gov provides tools and information, a way to ask questions and research brokers, and includes the mission of the SEC in ensuring fairness in the markets. There's a tab for proxy issues where the SEC explains "Your right to vote", "Voting Your Shares", "What You Should Do" and "How to Vote."

Some companies see the opportunity to engage with shareholders. Peggy Foran of Prudential Financial has taken a creative approach by offering retail shareholders who vote their proxies an environmentally correct tote with the Prudential logo. The proxy-voting shareholder can also opt for a donation to a charity—made by Prudential on the shareholder's behalf.

Not only will such a move encourage shareholders to vote, it signals the company's true desire to engage with shareholders.

Navigating this proxy season will not be easy, but companies that find creative ways to engage with their shareholders will improve their position and set the stage for the future.

SHAREHOLDERS HAVE GOVERNANCE RESPONSIBILITIES
NOVEMBER 20, 2009

In the aftermath of the financial crisis, there have been many proposals, as well as new rules and regulations to prevent its recurrence. Was it a failure of rules and regulations? What about our current rules, particularly those that apply to the way corporations are run?

Well-known and respected governance attorney Holly Gregory led a group of experienced lawyers (who reflect diverse shareholder, corporate and academic perspectives) in examining the roles and responsibilities of shareholders and boards under corporate law.

Their report, formally *Report of the Task Force of the ABA Section of Business Law Corporate Governance Committee on the Delineation of Governance Roles & Responsibilities* (aka "Governance Task Force") reflects a year of work and sets a constructive tone for boards, shareholders and policymakers to work together in strengthening corporate governance. The report reminds us that shareholders are not the only beneficiaries of the modern corporate system, which has created wealth on a scale previously unseen. The Governance Task Force report points out that corporations contribute to the public good by employing people, innovating, improving products and services, paying taxes, and by supporting various community and charitable programs that benefit society at large.

Anyone interested in corporate governance should read the report, not only for the detail of the legal constructs that have created our current system, but for granular detail in the footnotes complete with links that enable readers to follow their research and come to their own conclusions.

If you are looking for a scapegoat, there isn't one. Nor does a brush tar one group. Instead, the report describes how shareholders, management and boards have specific responsibilities to bring accountability to effective management and oversight.

The recommendations are logical. "Shareholders should act on an informed basis with respect to their governance-related rights…apply company-specific judgment when considering the use of voting rights…consider the long-term strategy of the corporation as communicated by the board in determining whether to initiate or support shareholder proposals."

Boards should "embrace their role as the body elected by shareholders to manage and direct the corporation by affirmatively engaging with shareholders to seek their views, consider shareholder returns and facilitate transparency." In addition they should "acknowledge at times the company's long-term goals and objectives may not conform to the desires of some of the shareholders." They should also "disclose with greater clarity how incentive packages are designed to encourage long-term outlook…"

Policymakers should, "in the context of reform initiatives", understand the rationale for the current roles and "carefully consider how to best encourage the responsible exercise of power by key participants in the governance of corporations so as to promote the long-term value creation…"

The report should be required reading for all shareholders.

ETHICS AND COMPLIANCE

IT'S THE 'DUMB QUESTIONS' THAT CAN SAVE THE COMPANY
MAY 7, 2011

Wayne Shaw encourages directors to ask "dumb questions" when it comes to reviewing the financials of any company. The Helmut Sohmen Distinguished Professor of Corporate Governance at Southern Methodist University notes that it is sometimes the question that wasn't asked that gives directors insight into assessing the integrity of the firm's financials.

His presentation was part of the NACD Professionalism training in Houston on May 4-6.

Rather than getting caught up in the minutia, directors should ask management, "Are we on track to meet our financial goals, and if not, what is the company doing about it?" He encourages directors to ask the CFO if he/she is comfortable with the financial demands of the CEO. "Is there pressure to make the numbers?"

Directors should ask internal auditors if they have any concerns with accounting or reporting issues. In following up with the external auditors, directors should ask how the company differs from others in the industry. What weaknesses did they find? How aggressive are the company's accounting policies relative to the competition? And finally, is management responsive to the issues they raise?

Shaw cited chapter and verse of well-known companies whose directors didn't ask the basic questions.

Asking some obvious questions would have saved millions of dollars of shareholders' investments, and in some cases, the company itself.

WHAT DIRECTORS CAN LEARN
FROM THE BP CRISIS
JULY 6, 2010

In his article in today's AgendaWeek, Stuart Levine makes a compelling case for directors to pay more attention to strategic communication and their understanding of reputational risk with the BP crisis as an example.

"Enterprise risk management is not limited to crisis situations. Establishing governance best practices to anticipate threats is a critical part of the challenges facing boards," he writes. And further, "To fulfill fiduciary responsibilities, questions and preparation both strengthen a company's ability to respond to unforeseen events."

Levine, a veteran board member and author of such best-selling business books as "Cut to the Chase", notes the need for board-level conversations and processes that review performance, risk and ethics.

MEMO TO CRISIS MANAGERS—FORGET CONTROL; THINK ENGAGEMENT
JUNE 30, 2010

The drama unfolding in the Gulf should send a strong message that the old playbook is inadequate for the social 24/7 always-on media.

What's still important: having a crisis plan. It can be as simple as a flow chart: How will you marshal your resources? Do you have a crisis web page ready to go live when the crisis hits? Do you have a well-defined process, a central point of contact for responding to questions and making decisions?

Begin by developing a set of principles. Live by them. Then, listen, engage and move forward with transparency.

While you want to be flexible about engaging and solving the problem, a number of key elements should already be in place: Do you have contacts lined up at the key stakeholders and influencer groups that are expected to be impacted the most in your crisis scenarios? And more importantly, do you have relationships with these stakeholders so that you can reach out to them early in the crisis to get input and help? Do you have internal contacts to proactively manage those relationships? Has your company/organization moved to a stance of engaging with key audiences early in resolving a crisis instead of facing off under the old-school confrontational approach?

Scenario planning is invaluable. One of the best guides remains "Shell Global Scenarios to 2025: The future business environment: trends, trade-offs and choices."

Ask for help. Form new alliances. Let your customers, employees, suppliers and community members tell you what's important.

You won't do everything right, but if you move forward guided by principles, you will be regarded as a decent member of the community.

LETTING SHAREHOLDERS AND THE GOVERNMENT
SHOULDER THE COST OF RISK
DECEMBER 30, 2009

Buyout firm founders are by nature risk-taking entrepreneurs. By making money for their clients, they create a loyal following, which Guy Hands, founder of buyout firm Terra Firma Capital Partners, has done. In his holiday letter he criticizes a system that has allowed "risk to be taken in the knowledge that, if things go right, bankers will take on average 60-80% of the profits generated through compensation and, if they go wrong, shareholders, and ultimately the Government, will pick up the costs."

Add to his remarks those made recently by National Economic Council director Larry Summers who said, "There is no financial institution that exists today that is not the direct or indirect beneficiary of trillions of dollars of taxpayer support for the financial system."

It would be wise for bank directors to consider these views when approving compensation plans.

DO THE RIGHT THING:
A KEY DIRECTOR RESPONSIBILITY
DECEMBER 8, 2009

Whether you are serving on a public or private company board, there is an important principle to guide you: do the right thing, not just for the constituency that brought you to the board, but for all the shareholders. This is according to Michel Feldman, partner in the Chicago office of Seyfarth Shaw, who has served on a number of private company and public boards.

"Especially when you are asked to be on a private board; be sure that you understand what you are getting into," said Feldman at an NACD Chicago panel. In private companies, it's especially important to beware of a dominant CEO.

"And always, do the right thing for all shareholders."

BOARD CONCERN IN HANDLING CRISES
OCTOBER 17, 2009

The McKinsey study showed that only half of the 186 directors who responded to their survey agreed that their boards met the demands of the crisis.

Such startling findings confirm that some directors are doing some soul searching.

The landscape has changed: shareholders, the government and regulators have demanded a higher standard for board performance. When a veteran board member and governance leader such as Barbara Hackman Franklin urges her directors to step up and become a force for improved governance, a sea change is underway.

Being a director has become a much more demanding job. And CEOs should be helping directors in

That's not an excuse to call in a host of consultants to solve the board's problems, but as the McKinsey article recommends, the board needs to take steps to be more effective.

REPUTATION

THE "PUBLICNESS" OF PUBLIC COMPANIES
APRIL 21, 2011

Those who work in corporate communications and public affairs have long held that companies must operate in the larger public interest. Now, Hillary Sale, a law professor at Washington University, has coined the new term "publicness" as she examines the Model Business Corporation Act and describes a set of responsibilities that U.S. companies need to better handle.

Communication professionals have pointed to Arthur W. Page, a PR executive for AT&T from 1927 to 1946 who developed a set of principles about how a company should operate, including "a successful corporation must shape its character in concert with the nation's. It must operate in the public interest, manage for the long run and make customer satisfaction its primary goal."

Professor Sale has used the law to describe how officers and directors of companies should act. In explaining the reason for creeping regulation she says, "The failure of officers and directors to govern in a sufficiently public manner has resulted not only in scandals, but also in more public scrutiny of their decisions, powers and duties." The government and the media, she says, are driven by the public, and now "have increasing influence over corporations, which requires a change in the way officers and directors understand and do their jobs."

CEOs and corporate directors would do well to read her excellent article in the Duke University journal, "Law and Contemporary Problems."

The bell has already been rung. The government and a larger public are involved in corporate governance and their concerns need to be addressed.

WHAT BP'S TONY HAYWARD NEEDS TO DO TO GET IT RIGHT
JUNE 8, 2010

Even with the containment cap placed over the ruptured oil well a mile deep in the Gulf, the live camera feed of the spewing oil creates a disturbing visual that represents the ineptitude of BP and Tony Hayward himself. Hayward, earnestly promising to "make it right," has become fodder for late night comedy.

Beyond stopping the leak from the well, what does Tony Hayward need to do to save BP's reputation and his own?

The gruesome images from the Gulf Shores, combined with the nearly incomprehensible size and scale of the disaster, only magnifies the extreme lack of control BP faced in managing this PR nightmare.

Hayward's biggest fault is not seeing the explosion and gushing well deep below the ocean's surface as an epic, global crisis. If Hayward had chosen to move beyond the legalese offered by counsel and his network of advisors, could he have said or done anything that would have improved his standing with the public? Did he have any good choices?

BP has been innovative in asking the public to help solve the problem, a laudable effort largely unrecognized. BP has received more than 20,000 ideas on how to stop the flow of oil or contain the oil spill. However, the promise to clean up every drop of oil and "restore the shoreline to its original state" appears as futile as the booms bobbing on the Gulf that barely contain the oil. As globs of oil foul the wetlands and the beaches, the company's commitment to meeting all of its responsibilities seems impossible to achieve.

The other media star of this drama, President Barack Obama, sought first to maintain distance between BP's gusher and his presidency. Reading the downward drift of the polls on his own leadership, he paraded his concern on Larry King Live, in a third visit to Louisiana, and in political briefings and radio addresses. Obama also promoted new regulations and ordered an investigation into BP's behavior.

What could each man have done differently—and do differently going forward—to gain credibility and respect? What positive developments can come out of the BP oil spill?

1. Hayward and Obama need to forge a new business/government relationship that stops the name-calling and blame-laying—one that instead conveys to a concerned public their shared dedication to solve the problem. On their own, they are each appealing for votes or applause or vindication, which the public finds insulting.

2. They must create a way for the public to participate in the solution. What programs can be put in place to engage the public in volunteerism related to the crisis? This type of work is cathartic for individuals who are grieving the loss of pristine coastlines and shorebirds. What's more, images of volunteer crews would supply positive, inspirational images to replace the current onslaught of disturbing images.

3. Obama must appoint an unassailable environmental leader—such as Bill Ruckelshaus—to develop energy policy that is green and business neutral. This individual must find innovative ways to invite participation and dialogue.

4. Invite the nations of the world to join together to create an environmental prize, based on solving or making progress in solving the world's greatest environmental problem—an environmental Nobel.

5. Create a new meaning for the British and U.S. relationship for the Fourth of July. Tony Hayward and BP should develop a unique participatory event for Americans on July 4th. Think big.

BUILDING TRUST THROUGH ENGAGEMENT
NOVEMBER 10, 2009

Senator Christopher Dodd (D-Conn) introduced his 1,135 page bill, Restoring American Financial Stability Act in the Senate Banking Committee with the goal of "creating a sound economic foundation to grow jobs, protect consumers, rein in Wall Street and prevent another financial crisis."

While many measures are drawn from Senator Charles Schumer's (D-N.Y.) Shareholder Bill of Rights, this greatly expands the scope.

Just last week, David Gergen, American political consultant and presidential advisor during four administrations, opined about the state of the economy at the Council of PR Firms' Critical Issues Forum according to Weber Shandwick's Chief Reputation Strategist, Leslie Gaines-Ross in her Reputation Exchange blog.

What a message for corporate boards to take the initiative to build trust by engaging with shareholders with effective board-shareholder communication programs.

PROTECT YOUR REPUTATION, DIRECTORS
OCTOBER 8, 2009

Being a director is an honor and a responsibility. An honor because it recognizes the individual's business accomplishments and the value he or she can bring to an organization in providing oversight. Directors also take on a heavy responsibility to use their judgment to serve the interests of shareholders.

"When you join a board, you put your reputation on the line," said Craig J. Duchossois, CEO of the Duchossois Group, a privately held company. "Do your due diligence on the company. Does the company share your values? Talk to management, other board members, employees, customers and the community." He made his remarks in a panel on Private Company Boards at a Chicago NACD meeting.

When Duchossois was asked how he did his due diligence, he turned to his newest board member in the audience, Donna Zarcone, and said, "Why don't you tell us, Donna."

"We did due diligence on each other," said Zarcone. "You have to. It's so important. With a private company, you want to look at everything that's available in the public realm. Then, you need to do a lot of private checking, with other board members, with management, employees, customers, the community. "

"Don't be shy about asking management for what you need to make a decision," added Michelle Collins, an advisory board member of Svoboda, Collins LLC, a private equity firm. "It's a great test of how the CEO treats his board members."

GOVERNANCE CHAMPIONS

BRITISH BOARDS: EVOLUTION OR REVOLUTION?
JULY 19, 2011

The SpencerStuart study, "Evolution or Revolution? Changes in Britain's boards of directors from 1960 to 2010", is an important contribution to the field of corporate governance. In crediting author Sir Geoffrey Owen for his role in telling the story, Mark Stroyan, Managing Director of Spencer Stuart, characterizes the history as both fascinating and important. As it illuminates the past, the study sets the stage for the discussion of how boards will continue to adapt in the future.

The search firm identified five concerns that boards need to address: 1) Preparing the next generation of chairmen with the caveat that not all CEOs are automatically suited to becoming chairmen, noting the critical skill of running a board meeting, drawing out and listening to all points of view, synthesizing the arguments and reaching conclusions without appearing to dominate. 2) The right of non-executives to seek advice because creating supplementary information channels is important for non-executive chairmen to discharge their duties in leading the board in oversight. 3) The pressure to appoint more women to boards has resulted in quotas in Norway. And while many protest that there aren't enough women with the relevant experience to serve, their view is that "there is a pool of potential candidates if boards are prepared to look less at proven general management experience and more at talent potential—to consider creative ideas and take some calculated risks."

While many sitting CEOs find it too time-consuming to sit on additional boards, Owen posits that 4) it is in the long-term interest of business that more working CEOs serve on boards. The 5th challenge is to create more engaged boards, but they note that when there are individuals in the boardroom who are really not contributing, it is "always uncomfortable to change the status quo" and ask the poor performing directors to leave.

One of the more interesting sidebars is "The Decline of the Guinea Pig," which described the job of an independent director as a "delightful perk for important (and often self-important) business folk at the end of their professional careers." These independents were "sometimes known as 'guinea pigs'—for a guinea and a free lunch they were happy to sleep through any chief executive's presentation of his corporate plan."

PRUDENTIAL LEADS IN
SHAREHOLDER ENGAGEMENT
MARCH 22, 2011

The Board of Prudential has repeated its strong corporate governance practice in filing its 2011 Proxy today. "As we did last year," says Peggy Foran, Chief Governance Officer, VP and Corporate Secretary, "the proxy begins with a three-page letter from the Board to shareholders. As we also did last year, we tried our best to 'plain English' in the proxy for easier reading for shareholders."

In addition, Prudential added a two-page summary to highlight business performance and compensation decisions. They incorporated suggestions from last year by including a chart on director experience and skills that the Governance Committee uses every year to evaluate the Board and recruit new board members.

At a time when so many boards are reluctant to engage with shareholders, Prudential is creating a template for best practices. As Peggy says, "Finding effective and innovative ways to communicate with shareholders is becoming increasingly vital. Shareholders need to be engaged. I see the future as engagement and communication."

RESTORING CAPITALISM THROUGH GOVERNANCE
FEBRUARY 17, 2011

"Business leaders today face a choice: We can reform capitalism, or we can let capitalism be reformed for us, through political measures and the pressures of an angry public," says Dominic Barton in his Harvard Business Review article.

The McKinsey global managing director has spent the past 18 months talking to more than 400 business and government leaders across the globe. He concludes that capitalism has been, and can continue to be, the greatest engine of prosperity ever devised. However, if the fundamental issues revealed in the recent crisis remain unaddressed and the system fails again, "the social contract between capitalism and the citizenry could rupture, with unpredictable but severely damaging results."

Barton confirms that boards must become more effective; they must represent a firm's owners and serve as the agent of long-term value creation. Being a director is also a much bigger job, as it requires more time and a deeper understanding of the company and its strategy. He makes many of the same points that Fred Steingraber and I make in our article in *Corporate Finance Review*, "What Boards Need to Do to Preserve Their Relevance and Provide Value in the World of the New Normal."

There is an urgency for management and boards to work together to fight the tyranny of short-termism, and "infuse their organizations with the perspective" that serving the interest of all stakeholders is essential to maximizing corporate value. Finally, boards need to be bolstered to govern like owners.

Inaction will produce the most negative consequences.

HOW BOARDS CAN REBUILD CONFIDENCE
FEBRUARY 18, 2010

When the former general counsel of the California Public Employees Retirement System (CalPERS) notes that boards need to assert strong, independent leadership and allow for increased dialogue between directors and shareholders, you know that the idea of real director engagement with shareholders has taken root.

In his opinion article in AgendaWeek, Richard Koppes discusses the ways directors can rebuild trust. Because Koppes served for 30 years and is a highly regarded expert in corporate governance, his words should reassure directors, especially those who began their service ten years ago.

In an article titled "Giving Boards Their Voice" from the new Korn Ferry International's *Briefings on Talent and Leadership,* I discuss the shift from behind-the-scenes advisors to highly accountable public figures. It is a profound transformation that boards are only beginning to grasp. The article discusses the importance of board-shareholder communication. By establishing independent communication, boards and their companies may succeed in quieting the dissent of shareholders and even winning the confidence of investors, which will enable companies to operate in the interests of the long term.

THE POWER OF AN INDIVIDUAL DIRECTOR
FEBRUARY 12, 2010

John Gillespie and David Zweig offer "solutions" to their indictment of corporate boards in their book, *Money for Nothing: How the Failure of Corporate Boards Is Ruining American Business and Costing Us Trillions.* In addition to their recommendations to split the chairman/CEO role, to allow shareholders to call an extraordinary general meeting, add some clout to say on pay, they cite individual, talented and committed directors who have helped to improve governance.

Jack Krol is cited for his role in helping Ed Breen to restore Tyco after the Kozlowski debacle. Ralph Whitworth is lauded for the ways he restored governance to Waste Management, and Michele Hooper is praised for her leadership in changing board culture and spreading those changes to multiple boards.

"Drawing on her early experience on Target's now legendary board beginning in the 1990s, Michele Hooper, a financial expert with a University of Chicago MBA, has brought those lessons to Warner Music Group, PPG Industries, AstraZeneca, UnitedHealth Group, Seagram and DaVita. Hooper learned from Target the value of having "a boardroom that allows for open and collegial discussion around the table without people getting upset or having a CEO who is going to put the kibosh on conversations."

Michele has modeled excellence and has been generous about sharing what she's learned. As the president of the Chicago chapter of the National Association of Corporate Directors, she volunteers her time to lead one of the strongest chapters of NACD, distinguished by its highly effective seminar programs. A board member of the national NACD, she facilitates training sessions for directors. In her day job, she is president and CEO of the Directors' Council, which finds candidates for boards.

By highlighting the impact of directors like Michele, the critics Gillespie and Zweig demonstrate that boards of directors are still our best hope for providing oversight to our management system.

A FINANCIAL ICON OFFERS AN AGENDA FOR RESTORING FAITH
JANUARY 19, 2010

John C. Bogle, the founder and former CEO of the Vanguard Group, cites a host of interesting statistics that document the changes in the investing public in his call for the creation of a Federation of Long-Term Investors, in which institutional investors, who alone hold some 15 percent of U.S. stocks, would join together to force changes in public company governance.

In his Wall Street Journal opinion article, Bogle quotes Leo Strine, vice chairman of the Delaware Court, who said, "No longer are the equity holders of public corporations diffuse and weak...they represent a new and powerful form of agency."

In the 2010 proxy season, boards of directors who develop programs of shareholder communication and active engagement with their owners will see better outcomes.

IT TAKES TIME TO BE AN EFFECTIVE DIRECTOR
DECEMBER 12, 2009

Bill McCracken joined CA, Inc. in 2005 as chairman of its Special Litigation Committee when the company was operating under a deferred prosecution agreement after it was rocked by scandals that included the conviction of several executives, including its CEO and Chairman, for fraud.

A case study in corporate rehabilitation, McCracken focused on the culture of CA, which he saw as a board responsibility. McCracken describes the continuation of the company's journey to excellence as "we're in the fifth chapter of a ten-chapter book."

In his panel discussion for the NACD Conference on Governance, McCracken also revealed that he believes the job of the lead director or chairman requires significant time—one and a half to two days a week or six or seven days a month.

Directors acknowledge a new environment where every director is spending more time on respective board assignments, especially the chairs of the audit or governance committees of the board.

McCracken took the unusual step of hiring an executive coach to help board members learn to work together and establish a company culture focused on transparency, teamwork and collaboration. "It takes time and effort to build trust."

McCracken also observed: You can't do both jobs—serving as chairman and CEO. He has taken over as interim CEO as they search for a new CEO.

"The Chairman runs and manages the board and the CEO runs the company."

Perhaps attending quarterly board meetings and an occasional telephonic meeting were the typical director time commitment a generation ago, but not today. Certainly, for the board to understand the risks in a corporate strategy means a much greater time commitment.

It's a bigger job today. Without an increased time commitment and an ability to work well together, "all that experience of the directors does not get engaged."

Clearly, management needs to take full advantage of directors and the experience they bring for the long-term growth and benefit to the company and its shareholders.

A CALL TO ACTION BY A KEY DIRECTOR
SEPTEMBER 15, 2009

Barbara Hackman Franklin has had an impressive career. The former U.S. Secretary of Commerce is a respected advocate and advisor to American companies doing business in international markets, notably China. She has been a director of 14 companies during her 25 years of service on corporate boards. Currently, she is a director at Aetna and Dow Chemical. In addition, she serves as the chairman of the National Association of Corporate Directors, the independent, non-profit organization whose 10,000 members represent the boards of companies from the Fortune 50 to smaller public companies, private companies, and nonprofit organizations.

In her opinion article in this week's Agenda, Franklin calls her fellow directors to action. "We, as directors, should simply step up to the new environment. Directors must demonstrate that we can make corporate governance more effective to serve the company and other stakeholders. I truly believe that more effective governance and more vigilance on our part can contribute significantly to a company's better financial and ethical performance."

She goes on to describe the two broad areas: first, she advises directors to rededicate themselves to understanding the companies they serve while renewing their own commitment to "integrity, good judgment, excellence and the courage to hold ourselves and company management to the highest standards."

Second, she advises directors to reevaluate how well board members work together as a group and whether the group works constructively with the CEO. And, if something needs fixing, "fix it."

The world has changed and boards need to step up, not complain about government involvement or the fact that shareholders have achieved power that boards must recognize and accommodate to make private enterprise better.

"We as directors have a responsibility to roll up our sleeves, do our jobs better and prove that private sector solutions remain the best way for American business to operate."

She urges directors to accept the NACD's principles for strengthening governance.

You will find that the 10th principle is shareholder communication, "Governance structures and practices should be designed to encourage communication with shareholders."

As Franklin says, it's time for directors to make the changes necessary to bring value to the companies they oversee and the shareholders they represent.

SIX SUGGESTIONS FOR DIRECTORS
SEPTEMBER 20, 2009

Welcomed warmly by fellow directors and friends at the opening NACD Chicago Chapter meeting on September 18th, Ed Liddy gave board members the benefit of his eleven-month stint as chairman and CEO of AIG, his one-dollar-a-year job that was called both hopeless and thankless by critics and supporters alike.

He had six suggestions.

First, he reminded them that being a board member is an honor, but it is also an enormous responsibility. Be sure that you understand the business at a fair level of detail.

Second, make sure that your risk management is married to a solid strategy. "Be prepared to challenge basic assumptions."

Third, don't let the structure of the organization become so complex that you don't understand it. "You always want to be able to say no."

Fourth, focus on succession planning, "not just for the CEO but for the top eight to ten leadership positions."

Fifth, understand leverage—not just financial leverage but investment leverage, product leverage and operating leverage.

Sixth, pay attention to make sure that you are getting the right information. "If you don't understand something, seek out more information from management through additional meetings or lunch, but never behind the back of the CEO."

After his brief remarks, commentator and nationally known personal financial expert Terry Savage interviewed Liddy and posed questions from the audience.

Liddy began his remarks by reminding the audience of the very difficult times of a year ago and how the financial system was in a very precarious state. "I had some relevant experience and I was asked to serve my country. I think most of you would have done it, too."

Thanking Liddy for his service, the audience rose in a standing ovation.

PRACTICING WHAT HE PREACHES
AUGUST 17, 2009

Proving that no good deed goes unpunished, Chairman Emeritus and CEO Emeritus of AT Kearney, Fred G. Steingraber became president of his village of Kenilworth last spring. Little did he know that problems with transformers exacerbated by turbulent summer thunderstorms would wipe out electricity for extended periods in this elite, North Shore village. Not only did Steingraber return every irate citizen's phone call, he also used the web in addition to newsletters to communicate what he, the town staff and ComEd were doing about the problem. In setting up a town meeting with ComEd, he scheduled it for October, not only to give ComEd time to resolve some of the issues, but to enable all interested citizens to attend without having to readjust their August vacation schedules.

Furthermore, he has also communicated about how trustees will fulfill their management roles going forward—he has published names of committee members and assignments, declared that all meeting materials will be delivered to board members ten days before the meeting to improve preparation and meeting effectiveness and efficiency.

Stephen Davis of the Millstein Center believes that "the single biggest motive for all the reforms of the past 25 years has been the sense of voicelessness and helplessness felt by major institutional investors." If directors are supposed to represent shareowners (at least in part), but they never communicate with shareowners, then owners become concerned when things aren't going well.

As Kenilworth village president, Steingraber's stakeholders are his friends and neighbors in a small, 3,000-person community. He honors them by lifting the veil from the management of the town's business. As a director of boards in the UK, Germany, India, Australia and the U.S., Fred has expressed concern over the government's increased involvement in board's activities.

Communication is one way that boards can retain and regain control rather than ceding to government through their silence.

SHAREHOLDER ENGAGEMENT

GET READY FOR FIFTH ANALYST CALL
FEBRUARY 24, 2011

A group of institutional investors has proposed a "Fifth Analyst Call" wherein U.S. public companies host a "dedicated conference call" in addition to the quarterly conference call for institutional investors focusing exclusively on corporate governance matters with the primary dialogue between investors and directors.

Mindful of Regulation Full Disclosure, the call would be scheduled 10 to 15 days before the annual meeting and would cover material that is in the proxy. While every company will need to examine its particular needs, this proposal is a framework that encourages dialogue.

Directors should embrace this opportunity to efficiently communicate with institutional investors and beneficial owners with the ability to interact directly with shareholders not filtered through proxy advisory firms or solicitors.

Yes, it will require preparation. But shouldn't those who are paid to represent the interest of shareholders be able to discuss the company's governance framework and philosophy, the board's structure, effectiveness and succession planning? Directors should be able to discuss the internal controls and risk management practices and even answer questions about executive compensation.

Such dialogue could be enormously helpful to boards at this critical time in helping to restore trust in their work in providing governance oversight.

DISCLOSURE VERSUS ENGAGEMENT
APRIL 19, 2011

My position of suggesting that companies refine the concept of the Fifth Analyst Call to improve upon the proposal by a group of institutional investors (and thereby limiting the benefit to the interests of this coalition) to make it a fair process that corporate managers can properly use to serve all investors equally has drawn some interesting reactions.

John Wilcox, the Chairman of Sodali commented that, "directors of U.S. companies are not ready for open dialogue with their investors, even on a narrowly defined topic such as corporate governance and the annual meeting. The reason they are not ready is because U.S. companies—and boards in particular—are generally on the defensive in their communication with shareholders. Instead of communication, U.S. companies practice disclosure. Disclosure is defined by prescriptive rules and enforced by liability and regulatory penalties." This, he says, makes "boards and shareholders mistrustful of each other and relies on adversarial modes of engagement."

Boards guided by legal counsel continue to respond by addressing the "letter of the law", grudgingly meeting new demands for transparency rather than the spirit of the law, which Mary L. Schapiro, SEC Chairman, emphasized as "true engagement with shareholders."

In this environment, Washington will continue to regulate, with many unintended consequences until CEOs and their boards see shareholders as part of the governance process and critical to not only their long-term health but the health of capitalism in the 21st century.

DIRECTORS, YOUR JOB IS TO EFFECTIVELY ENGAGE WITH SHAREHOLDERS
OCTOBER 20, 2010

Mary L. Shapiro, SEC Chairman, was as plain-spoken and direct as she could be in addressing the 600 plus directors at the National Association of Corporate Directors annual conference. She thanked them for inviting her to speak at a time when "so much about what you do—and what I do—is being fundamentally transformed."

"Speaking both as a regulator and as a former board member, I believe that it is vital that shareholders and board members move beyond the minimum required communications and become truly engaged in the shared pursuit of high quality governance.

"For boards and their companies, engagement means more than just disclosure. It means clear conversations with investors about how the company is governed—and why and how decisions are made.

"But engagement is a two-way street. Boards can also benefit from access to the ideas and the concerns investors may have. Good communications can build credibility with shareholders and potentially enhance corporate strategies."

It wasn't surprising then that the first question during the Q&A asked about running afoul of Regulation FD. As she has said in the past and repeated, "Reg FD doesn't present a barrier to director-shareholder communication. We have provided additional guidance to directors such as pre-clearing conversations, imposing no-trading restrictions on the shareholders who are talking to directors. In short, Regulation FD is not meant to be a barrier."

In conclusion she noted that, "Technology, investor attitudes and the way financial markets work have all changed dramatically during the past decade. The way in which we, and in which you and your shareholders communicate, must similarly change.

"The SEC cannot, and is not interested in, determining the communications strategies of individual companies. But we are interested in breaking down barriers that may prevent effective engagement, and affect investor confidence and, ultimately, financial performance."

Boards should be developing communication plans now, re-examining their governance documents in light of the changing environment and developing strategies to contribute to improve governance.

EVEN LAWYERS ARE TELLING DIRECTORS, IT'S TIME TO COMMUNICATE
SEPTEMBER 1, 2010

During a webinar, *DC in the Boardroom: A Board Level Briefing on Proxy Access,* the three attorney panelists (David Caplan and Annette Nazarath, partners at Davis Polk and Wardell, John Gorman, partner at Luse Gorman, http://www.luselaw.com/gorman.html and former Special Counsel, Division of Corporation Finance and former SEC Commissioner) all agreed that directors should enhance their communication with shareholders. They also agreed that the time to act is now.

During this period leading up to the proxy season, directors should be engaging in some form of self-evaluation to understand what their vulnerabilities are. Do shareholders have concerns about executive compensation, the capabilities of the current board of directors or other governance issues?

Nazareth, a former SEC Commissioner, reminded the participants that "investor protection has been a focus of the SEC, and one way of ensuring protection is good corporate governance."

Directors should "consider ways to enhance shareholder communication so that you're not in the position of your 3% shareholders feeling that they need to nominate their own directors because they are not being represented appropriately by the current board."

DIRECTORS, DO YOU HAVE A SHAREHOLDER ENGAGEMENT PROGRAM?
AUGUST 12, 2010

With the passage of the Dodd-Frank Wall Street Reform and Consumer Protection Act, power has shifted to shareholders. The 2011 proxy season is a game-changer as the rules require boards to seek shareholder support for compensation programs and even directorship candidates.

Directors, do you have a shareholder engagement program? Have you reviewed and assessed the board capacity for shareholder communication and dialogue? Have you discussed how you will handle increased dialogue and interaction with shareholders?

The board world has changed. Shareholders have greater power to influence board composition and executive pay based on the provisions of Dodd-Frank for proxy access, say on pay, and limits on broker discretionary voting.

By remaining silent, boards increase the power of proxy advisors as the only independent guidance to shareholders on how to vote. Boards increasingly need to engage with key shareholders, initiating communication and dialogue.

Get started now.

CRITICAL NEED FOR BOARDS TO UNDERSTAND
THEIR SHAREHOLDERS
AUGUST 1, 2011

It's clear that say on pay is not going away. For companies whose shareholders rejected or expressed concern about the executive compensation programs with large numbers of negative votes, now is the time for boards to create a strategy to engage with shareholders to better understand their concerns.

Compensation consultant Robin Farracone of Farient Advisors warns boards not to "just sit there and do nothing" because it invites opposition to grow. Let it fester, she says, and it places the board and the company in a negative spotlight that "creates reputational damage and could even have a depressive effect on the stock price."

Boards have been reluctant to engage with shareholders because they often don't have a picture of what a board engaging with shareholders might look like. Often, they believe it is the job of the investor relations department. But say on pay focuses on the board's role in approving compensation programs for the named officers for the company. And shareholders expect the board to be responsive.

"Good engagement takes different forms, but it's critical to get an early start," says Patrick McGurn of ISS, also interviewed in the "Corporate Secretary" article. The Dodd-Frank requirement for say on pay voting was designed to encourage dialogue between the board and shareholders. Some boards, like Prudential, established a dedicated compensation committee email address and actively seek electronic queries on pay matters and anything else related to board work. Prudential regularly sends board members and representatives on engagement exercises with investors.

Not only should board members be able to demonstrate that the compensation program is aligned with performance, they should also be able to explain compensation in general terms. This has proven to be a difficult task that directors should correct by requiring themselves to explain in plain English.

GOLDMAN DECIDES IT'S A GOOD IDEA TO COMMUNICATE WITH SHAREHOLDERS
APRIL 7, 2010

In advance of its May 7th annual meeting with shareholders, Goldman Sachs used surprising candor in an eight-page letter in its 2009 annual report. Reiterating that it didn't 'bet against' clients by using short positions that it took on before the residential real estate market crashed. Rather, it was one of the first Wall Street firms to reduce its real estate exposure, "even as some clients were sticking with their bullish bets."

The Financial Times concludes, "The [note] is an implicit admission that Goldman's long-held strategy of giving short shrift to criticism of its behavior and pay policies during the crisis has done little to quell the public backlash against the Wall Street bank."

After such a mea culpa, how will Goldman Sachs handle its annual meeting? Will it be a Kabuki show or will Chairman and CEO Lloyd Blankfein lead his directors in a sincere effort to engage with shareholders? Blankfein has a chance to demonstrate that he's committed to minimizing reputation risk by making the meeting a true opportunity for shareholders to question and receive genuine responses from him and the board of directors.

It's a dramatic change and they should be preparing now.

PRUDENTIAL SETS A NEW STANDARD FOR COMMUNICATION WITH SHAREHOLDERS
MARCH 16, 2010

Not only does Prudential Financial prove that the proxy can serve as an effective communication vehicle to shareholders while fulfilling its legal requirement, the company has also added a number of innovations that set new standards for others.

It begins with the Letter from the Board of Directors to our Shareholders: "As stewards of the Company, we are committed to governing Prudential in an effective and transparent manner. We hold ourselves to high standards with respect to governance "best practices" and we believe that communicating with you on significant matters is an important part of our obligation to align governance and management with the best interests of shareholders."

The letter summarizes both the way the board has been responsive to shareholders and items that will be explained in depth in the proxy. The letter enables the board to highlight its shareholder-friendly approach, including the advisory vote on executive compensation, the special financial award to 15,000 employees, clawbacks, the board's active engagement in succession planning and how it has approached risk oversight.

It also invites shareholders to write to the board and provides email addresses for independent directors as well as a website for feedback on executive compensation. How simple and effective.

The proxy does a nice job of describing the current board and their qualifications, as well as outlining a process for selecting directors, including an explanation of how shareholders can recommend director candidates. The board explains its process and philosophy for compensation.

Best of all, it's in plain English—clear, readable and understandable.

NEW RULES REQUIRE BETTER
BOARD COMMUNICATION
DECEMBER 17, 2009

"By adopting these rules, we will improve the disclosure around risk, compensation, and corporate governance, thereby increasing accountability and directly benefiting investors," Chairman Mary Schapiro said in her opening statement at yesterday's Securities and Exchange meeting.

The rules will be in effect by the 2010 proxy season and could be published as early as next week.

Do boards understand that they are being challenged to communicate more openly with their shareholders? Better communication gets to the heart of many of the governance issues that the SEC and the pending legislation hope to address.

So what's a board to do?

Boards should think in concrete terms about what they have communicated with their shareholders in the past and how they can improve the clarity of communication. They should avoid legalese and adopt plain English in their discussion about risk, compensation and governance.

Greater disclosure is about clarity. Boards are in a communication battle they can win if they recognize the element of respect in their communication with the company's owners.

LEADERSHIP

LEADERSHIP LESSONS FROM
GENERAL DAVID PETRAEUS
MAY 19, 2010

While addressing a crowd of 1,500 at the Chicago Council of Global Affairs Tuesday night at the Fairmont Hotel in Chicago, General David Petraeus, U.S. Central Commander, translated his leadership lessons in battle for the boardroom and management.

Corporate leaders need to be strategic. "They need to get the big ideas right." For Petraeus, the big idea that the US military got right was a surge, not just in troops but in ideas, to change the war the U.S. was in danger of losing in Iraq. The second requirement is to educate and communicate the big ideas or the strategies to those in your command—the troops or the workers. One of the things Petraeus expected of his troops down to the private on the street was to respect the rights of the Iraqi citizens, even those under arrest. This "live your values" approach was part of the critical task of securing the population. The third lesson is to oversee the implementation of the big ideas by utilizing effective feedback mechanisms. And the fourth lesson is to not micromanage. Within that is the requirement to capture the best practices and kill the bad practices.

This four-star general, a Ranger, a Ph.D. from Princeton's Woodrow Wilson School whose doctoral thesis challenged not only the conventional thinking on the Vietnam War but the prevailing strategies about war itself. "This is not a 'take the hill, plant the flag' kind of war," Petraeus said.

Communication is at the core of his leadership style. "Be first with the truth," he says. He is quick to distil leadership lessons and write about them as he did listing 14 lessons learned in training the Iraqi army.

Petraeus showed two slides in his presentation—one was a chart that graphed the number of violent incidents in Iraq on a weekly basis, a dramatic visual of how bad it was and how the violence has subsided. The second was a photograph of a re-enlistment ceremony—thousands of young Americans re-enlisting after hard campaigns. "I want to close by thanking you for your support of our troopers. It's critical. They re-enlisted not only because they believe it's right and they're making a difference but because you appreciate what they're doing."

Americans are lucky that David Petraeus is Commander of CentCom and the most admired military thinker in the world today.

BILL RUCKELSHAUS LOOKS BACK,
OFFERS ADVICE GOING FORWARD
APRIL 19, 2010

William Ruckelshaus describes how the U.S. got serious about environmental issues with the creation of the Environmental Protection Agency 40 years ago in his Saturday commentary in the Wall Street Journal. The turning point from the "race to the bottom" came when the public demanded action.

If that's where shareholders and the larger public are today on corporate governance issues, directors should take notice. The top-down, standard-setting enforcement process of the 1970s isn't going to fix the more complex issues today. He concludes that "people affected by change have to be deeply involved in crafting solutions" and "we have to get better at both involving people in the process of change and providing them with enough information to make that involvement useful and worthwhile."

While he's talking about environmental issues, couldn't that be applied to boards and shareholders?

As Bonnie Hill has observed in her years as a director engaging with shareholders, "We have learned so much from our interaction with shareholders. It has made us better directors."

The world has changed. We can't fight the last war or use yesterday's solutions to solve today's problems. The new tools include more direct engagement with shareholders, not to pacify them but to involve them in the long-term investment of our companies.

THE LEADERSHIP STYLE OF STEVEN JOBS
OCTOBER 11, 2011

The iBooks will be appearing on iPads (and Kindles) shortly: how the leadership style of Steven P. Jobs created the most valuable company in the world.

The obituaries reminded us that this was the man who transformed the way we use technology, how we listen to music, watch TV shows and movies. Not only a genius, Steve Jobs will be remembered as the leading figure of our time.

Jobs saw himself as neither a hardware engineer nor a software programmer, but a technology leader who chose the best people possible. And once they worked for him, he encouraged them, yes, but more often he prodded and criticized them. Occasionally, he even humiliated those who dared to bring him anything short of "insanely great."

Be careful, leadership gurus, how you spin these critical characteristics. In anyone less than Steve Jobs, that is, all of us, such insistence on being better, not settling for less could turn harsh, and brutal.

Steve Jobs meddled, demanded that everyone do better. Steve Jobs, who suffered his own purgatory at a young age, grew success outside of Apple and returned to create greater triumphs in recreating the company; he embodied the gifts and the knowledge to elicit extraordinary loyalty.

"He was the most passionate leader one could hope for, a motivating force without parallel," wrote Steven Levy, author of the 1994 book "Insanely Great," which chronicles the creation of the Mac.

GOVERNANCE

THE BUSINESS CASE FOR GOOD GOVERNANCE
JULY 6, 2009

In the wake of the economic collapse and the devastating impact of risky behavior by management in companies like Citigroup and Countrywide, corporate boards are paying more attention to their responsibility for oversight. While most of the problems developed in the financial sector, boards in other sectors are naturally concerned, especially as they watch mounting legislation in Washington.

That's why smart boards are getting ahead of the curve. Even if the U.S. Chamber of Commerce issues a statement saying that it is "disturbed by the change" to eliminate broker discretionary voting, smart boards are preparing for the 2010 proxy season. Rather than railing against an activist Securities and Exchange Commissioner, most directors recognize underlying shareholder concerns. They are serious about good governance because it's a business value.

INCREASING PROXY VOTING CAN
BEGIN WITH EMPLOYEES
APRIL 1, 2011

In his remarks before the National Press Club, Broadridge CEO Richard J. Daly called for a nationwide effort to encourage employees to vote their proxies and thereby participate in the larger enterprise of improving corporate governance.

As we said in our tweet earlier today (Karen Kane @BoardAdvisor), Daly is right to use his position to encourage shareholder education by asking the country's top 1000 CEOs to mobilize employees to participate in corporate governance by voting their proxies.

Daly calls Broadridge the major player in investor communications and proxy distribution, providing the digital pipes for these transactions, but he also notes that Broadridge makes no more or less money from an increased exercise of proxies.

Companies and the boards of directors that provide oversight need to embrace the concept that engaging shareholders has never been more important in restoring trust. Shareholders need to be reminded that their proxy represents their investment, their wealth and their financial returns.

"It is clear to me that when raising capital, creating jobs and effectively competing in an increasingly global market, companies need input and support from shareholders to validate they are on the right track."

BOARDS SHOULD LEAD GOVERNANCE IMPROVEMENTS
NOVEMBER 15, 2009

With unprecedented interest in corporate governance, the Chicago NACD Chapter panel of Holly Gregory, Fred Steingraber, Donna Zarcone and William Atwood addressed *Changes in Regulation and Implications for Directors.*

Panelist Fred Steingraber, former Chairman and CEO of AT Kearney and director of several US and several international boards, said the time for boards to react was over. Rather, boards should take a leadership position by demonstrating that they provide value with their oversight through transparency and better shareholder communication.

"Boards are in the midst of a very serious struggle to regain respect and control over their growing responsibilities and image," said Steingraber. "To accomplish this will require demonstrating the will and capacity to make changes ranging from board organization/leadership, policy, process, committees, board composition to shareholder communications. They must now demonstrate leadership at the board level with a results orientation in the conduct of their work.

"Today, the government is taking control of boards, largely due to directors not building good relations with shareholders and all too frequently being too defensive and too reactive in their communication."

Boards need to break their silence to retain and regain control rather than ceding authority to critics.

"Not only do boards need to listen to shareholders to understand their concerns, they also need to go beyond the derivative information that they normally receive to drill down to the underlying issues of business performance," said Steingraber. "Boards need to put together a longer term program that addresses the issues of succession planning and risk management. This will not happen overnight." For that reason boards need to lead by creating a framework for change and communicate those changes, which will take place over time."

LESSONS FROM PRIVATE EQUITY BOARDS
OCTOBER 15, 2009

In a presentation at the International Association of Interim at the Four Seasons today, Prism Capital partner Stephen Vivian spoke about the unique nature of private equity boards. "The independent directors of private equity boards are much more immersed in active engagement with management, coaching them, mentoring them as they focus relentlessly on business strategy."

Often characterized as "player-coaches," these independent directors play an important role in taking the company to the next level. "We find that the CEOs of these companies listen better to these independent directors because they've been there—they've run a business; they've been successful. They can make enormous contributions as mentors. However, the independent board members don't work for the PE firm but rather have a fiduciary duty to act in the best interest of the company."

In the best of all worlds, engagement, focus on strategy and commitment to one's fiduciary duty are qualities that directors of private equity and corporate boards share.

RAM CHARAN'S ADVICE TO CORPORATE BOARDS
AUGUST 12, 2009

What has fueled the activism of shareholders in the past 25 years? We know that periods of flat or negative growth, flat or negative profitability and low stock growth can drive traditionally passive institutional shareholders to activism. (In fact, according to Shareholder Activism Insight, the likelihood is 79 percent.)

But long-time participants and observers in the corporate governance community think it's much more basic: it's a sense of voicelessness and helplessness felt by major institutional investors. These shareholders believe they suffer from lack of access—to the directors, to information. This "under-representation" feeds some activists' demands to be recognized as owners, whether it's advocating for say on pay, majority voting, or even a battle for board seats.

If directors seem confused by the criticism, it's because many believe they have been in full disclosure through legal documents properly filed: the 8K, the 10K, the proxy, the governance documents posted on the company's website. But in an era of transparency can boards afford to remain in the background?

The NACD's "Key Agreed Principles to Strengthen Corporate Governance for U.S. Publicly Traded Companies" was universally endorsed by the director community. But how many boards have designed "governance structures and practices" to "encourage communication with shareholders"? And what would it look like?

Shareholders have a legitimate interest in the governance of their companies. What are the issues for your shareholders? How has the board addressed those issues?

Here are some points to keep in mind, courtesy of Ram Charan, "the go-to advisor for corporate directors and CEOs."

- Shareholder activism is here to stay. Boards need to change their psychology to see it as a constructive influence, not a nuisance.
- Boards must be prepared to communicate directly with shareholders when the situation warrants.
- Shareholders want the board to hear their concerns, but boards must be independent and sometimes push back.

THE SIMPLE TRUTH OF WINNING INVESTORS OVER
NOVEMBER 17, 2011

In a webinar sponsored by the Harvard Business Review, Baruch Lev, professor of Accounting and Finance at the Stern School of Business of New York University, debunked a number of favorite investor myths, not with opinions but with quantitative research.

The webinar is based on Lev's latest book, *Winning Investors Over: Surprising Truths about Honesty, Earnings Guidance, and Other Ways to Boost Your Stock Price.* He points out that capital markets are crucial to companies' success and those who lead them. But corporate leaders are largely mired in misconceptions that govern their behavior to the detriment of employees, investors and interested parties. Perhaps one of the biggest myths is that investors are focused on short-term, quarter-to-quarter results.

Instead, Dr. Lev presents detailed research that charts how investors are patient and have strongly supported long-term growth investments from 1947 to 2007.

The bromide to winning this battle is honest, regular communication with investors coupled with conservative accounting. He advises companies to go beyond required disclosure to enhance investor understanding. And actions such as corporate leaders increasing their personal investment in a company also go a long way to convey credibility. "Share some knowledge. Let your investors know what's in the pipeline of products."

By challenging conventional wisdom and backing it up with research, Baruch Lev gets it right.

ABOUT THE AUTHOR

Karen Kane is a shareholder engagement strategist and National Association of Corporate Directors Governance Fellow. In her work with corporate and non-profit boards, she assists in helping CEOs and boards gain direct control of communication with investors through shareholder engagement, developing channels to receive shareholder intelligence, and incorporating shareholder feedback on key issues.

Ms. Kane is a communications leader and advocate for the use of strategic communication as a risk mitigation tool in today's complex business environment. She has written extensively on the topic of leadership responsibility and good governance.

A former board secretary and highest ranking woman at the Federal Reserve Bank of Chicago, Ms. Kane is a C-Suite communication advisor who has built a practice of assisting CEOs in all aspects of executive communication. She has served as a senior corporate officer in diverse business segments including environmental, high-tech, insurance, the media, banking and asset management.

An experienced crisis manager, she led the development of the crisis communication plan for the Federal Reserve System after the attacks of 9/11. She is an NACD Governance Fellow, offering communication assistance to CEOs and boards on a wide array of shareholder engagement and governance issues.

INDEX